Tobey Gross

POWER DYNAMICS AND EMOTIONAL INTELLIGENCE: SIMPLIFIED PERSPECTIVES

A Handbook on Scientific Foundations and
Principles in Language Proficiency,
Communication and Social Psychology

Volume 3

MINKOWSKI
Institute Press

Dr. Tobey Gross
Professor of Educational Science
www.tobeygross.de

ISBN: 978-1-998902-39-2 (softcover)
ISBN: 978-1-998902-40-8 (ebook)

Minkowski Institute Press
Montreal, Quebec, Canada
http://minkowskiinstitute.org/mip/

For information on all Minkowski Institute Press publications
visit our website at http://minkowskiinstitute.org/mip/books/

This book series is dedicated to my parents.

PREFACE

This handbook serves as a supportive resource for higher education courses in communication sciences and language proficiency. While it is not intended to be exhaustive, it focuses on theories and concepts, that I, through my own experience in higher education, find especially valuable.

The understanding and application of the knowledge in this book have repeatedly shown to contribute to the aforementioned fields.

The domain of communication is fast-paced and ever-evolving, as well as it plays a significant role in a myriad of scientific fields, such as psychology, general language education or management.

Dr. Tobey Gross
Professor of Educational Science
www.tobeygross.de

ii

FOREWORD

The current era is marked by fast-paced, multi-faceted, global, cross-cultural communication on a daily basis, and communicative studies are rightfully part of many programs in higher education. I have taught a number of differently-focused language education programs and have read countless brilliant works on the matter. However, there are several common denominators, as well as there is probably an essence of what the most influential aspects in communication sciences are, that should be considered and respected in interdisciplinary domains. This book aims to serve as a resource for what I consider the essential theories and concepts, that crucially contribute to the broader domain of language proficiency. These selections are based on my personal experience in educative environments, and there are certainly a whole lot more excellent frameworks and concepts on the topic. The chosen content reflects a blend of theoretical knowledge and equally its practical applicability, hence the term *"handbook"* – attempting to integrate the essential insights from psychology, rhetoric and cultural studies, as well as pragmatics and discourse analysis.

While it is certainly meant to be material especially tailored to educators and students, I deliberately tried to maintain a digestible language throughout this work, so any interested reader would have the opportunity to draw their conclusions and understand the key takeaways.

iv

CONTENTS

Introduction to Communication Sciences and Language Proficiency

The multidimensional nature of language proficiency

In characterizing, what language proficiency consists of, we must first eliminate the misconception, that it only means the correctness and fluency of a language. There is much more to the topic of language proficiency than only correct grammar and a well-established lexical range.

There are different approaches to the definition, because there has been no general consensus about what characterizes a general language proficiency in a way that would have suited each and every scenario. Therefore, we want to perceive it as multidimensional in nature.

Aspects of language proficiency

The Council of Europe (2001) acknowledges linguistic, cognitive and sociocultural factors for a broader definition. ACTFL for example, define common denominators, that have to be fulfilled, in order to reach different levels of language proficiency. Other than that, they agree with the broader consensus, that language proficiency is mostly defined by the four core competency domains listening, speaking, reading and writing (ACTFL, 2012).

A broader conceptual framework has been defined by Kern in 2000, who integrates further components into the assessment of language proficiency, one which I personally find more suitable, or at least, more global and exhaustive. Kern defines linguistic components, under which I count all of the aforementioned, but further he states, that cultural awareness and nuances, as well as the ability of critical thinking must be acknowledged in the regard of overall language proficiency (Kern, 2000).

Capturing in-depth psychological underpinnings

My framework that I typically use for the introduction of language proficiency - you could see it as my introductory lecture in higher education - is simple and at the same time, it captures the essential aspects, that I like to treat in a course. As I already mentioned earlier, this is my personal experience and I do not claim to reinvent the wheel here, nor do I feel like my personal approach outperforms another; I am sharing experience-based knowledge, hopefully to some peers' inspiration and enrichment. No more, no less.

Students will have to master linguistic concepts, of course, so correctness and fluency form the foundation of any respective course. Stage I is essentially meant for getting rid of grammar mistakes and misconceptions, raising metalinguistic awareness and making them aware of interlingual interference in morphology and syntax. To me, mastery of those concepts is the basic foundation of anything that is to follow, hence I assess and fly through the commonly troublesome grammar topics while at the same time I do my best to increase the lexical range.

However, this book focuses on the second stage, and in some ways I do consider it the one that makes for a much larger part of actual language proficiency. Stage II is characterized by knowledge about social cognition and psychology: the behavioral side of language, if you will, and this is where lectures get engaging, interesting, and language becomes a real powerful tool. Stage III eventually forms the synthesis of the former two, using the tools from Stage I and the building blocks from Stage II, in order to actually build. Now obviously, Stage II has a lot of content to it, and there might never be an exhaustive list of what is to be considered important, so in the following chapters, I will delve into those frameworks and concepts in psychology, general rhetoric, pragmatics and social cognition, that I consider especially valuable for students in language proficiency courses.

Language as a coherent system of different disciplines

Language, in communication sciences, is to be perceived as not only forming correct morphology and syntax, but is a much broader field, that only comes to life in social context. Hence, I consider the psychosociological underpinnings of language at least as important as the actual stage of fluency and development of a lexical range and correct inflection. There is a necessary integration of a so-called observer perspective in behavior and context to the application of language, which makes for a large part in its proficient use (Pike, 1982). Furthermore, nonverbal communication should not fall into the cracks, either. It is an important aspect when speaking of language proficiency, as we will later see, since it makes for the even largest part of actual communication (Mehrabian, 1972). Apart from that, sociolinguistics teach us, that social conventions, participant status and many different cultural norms and other aspects contribute to language proficiency (Hymes, 1972). Discourse analysis and strategic competencies, which, on the one hand, I'd rather consider part of the synthesis, but on the other, need to be introduced in context, should at least be mentioned in this introduction's regard.

Since later, from correctness in grammar, fluency style, over psychological knowledge and awareness of sociological cues, and bridging it all into style, behavior and application, it forms some sort of a flow, they cannot always be explicitly and sharply divided anyhow (Canale & Swain, 1980).

1 FOUNDATIONS OF POWER DYNAMICS

1.1 "A Simplified Perspective" – Why?

Power Dynamics alone might already be the most complex topic that I want to touch upon within this book series, and treating it in an exhaustive manner would not only escalate way beyond the digestible amount of information in the manner of which this book shall be written. It would also have to provide a vast amount of information, that, in the context of higher education in communication and language proficiency, is irrelevant. That does not mean, that the topic of Power Dynamics is of less importance than the other ones, but it is quite extensive and much of the underlying knowledge would be excessive for educators and students likewise, in the context of what this book series is meant for.

Now, that I have chosen to add Emotional Intelligence to complete this volume, it even more so demands a simplified and downscaled treatment.

Power Dynamics is a topic, that, when treated and investigated exhaustively, would fill more than the entire series, and I will admit, that before the decision to simplify the perspective, I spent some weeks trying to make an outline that contained much more of the historical developments and original theories and research. It was, when I gathered my literature, that I grew aware of how extensive the load of topics would really become, and the first thing I did subsequently,

1

was to split Emotional Intelligence and Power Dynamics, so that this would be a standalone topic.

When the final outline was completed, I did what I always do with a publishment; I left myself some days and took a mental distance, so that I could come back and look at it after some cognitive detachment. After that, I could not have been more dissatisfied with my outline, because I had a sense of *"boredom"*, if you will. Not because the topic of Power Dynamics felt boring to me, on the contrary. But the extensive outline gave me the impression, that it would become really exhausting to read and to establish a mental connection between the philosophical foundations and the historical development of Power Dynamics and the many different perspectives it offers, and the purpose of this book series.

I had to make a decision. I would either discard the topic for the time being, and work on something else, or I would entirely restructure my idea of the book. The latter I did. Thus, this work, after some careful consideration, contains a core version of Power Dynamics, the basics that form a distinct understanding, and additionally, Emotional Intelligence, tailored to the very purpose of the entire series. I have made sure, that the core of comprehending power and hierarchy through communication sciences, and the applicability (not at least) through Emotional Intelligence, are tailored to a practical use in the realm of higher education courses of language proficiency and communication psychology.

The other main reason for simplification is, that historical theories on power and hierarchy are particularly complex and thus, might be difficult to grasp. Contextualizing them makes more sense in my opinion, and as a resource for practical applicability, it is a good idea to simplify the historical context to an extent that will not take away the core, but does not escalate beyond the boundaries of what is really needed to apply it to modern settings and communication scenarios.

Note: simplification extends to the scope of treated subchapters, but not to the depth with which each topic is treated. While the number of chapters and subtopics is limited to the essential, providing sufficient depth of each is paramount by all means.

1.2   The Evolution of Power Concepts

In this chapter, I will introduce the most influential and seminal concepts of power that were born from the ideas of thinkers who sustainably impacted our understanding of power, and whose theories have had seminal influence until the present day. The concepts I will present have been the foundation for many further explorations throughout the past decades, and therefore, we will aim to understand what made them so influential to begin with.

In my opinion, it makes sense to keep a topical order among the presented individuals and their theories, so I will start with Robert Dahl. In his work *"Who Governs?"* (1961) Dahl challenged a then-prevailing perception of power, which was defined by the belief, that power in American cities was concentrated in the hands of an elite ruling class, that functioned as a controlling unity. The majority had believed, that all political power was highly centralized. Dahl conducted investigations of power structures in the political landscape through case studies, analyses of policies and public decisions and was able to show, that the prevailing notion of a concentrated power was incorrect. Rather than being centralized within an elite of few, power was much more complex and competitive, distributed among various groups with differing interests. Dahl observed, that in a democratic society, the plurality of competing interest groups held a multifaceted and dynamic form of power.

An interesting question to ask would be, why the majority of society had had this perception of a concentrated power, when in reality, that was not the case at all. When carefully studying Dahl's work, we grow aware of how perception and reality can drift apart in such regard, specifically under the preassumption, that a felt ruling elite is almost always perceived as negative and sometimes even oppressive.

Moving on in the timeline of power concepts, one of the most influential works of all time shapes the respective discourse until the present day. French and Raven (1959) presented five distinct types of power, that can be perceived as "timeless", because they are applicable in many scenarios and regardless of the era they are applied to. The main difference between Dahl's work and French and Raven's work is the subject: Dahl concentrated his investigations on governing power, which limited his scope to politics, while French and Raven paid attention to organizations. They carefully analyzed interactions in various entities, and identified five different base types of power that they concluded were essential for effective leadership and management. These five types are *reward, coercive, legitimate, referent and expert* power.

Reward power is the one that holds the capability of distributing rewards or positively perceived action, hence holding an influence to those that expect being rewarded.

Quite the opposite would be *coercive* power, which is held by individuals who possess the capability to punish or distribute repressive or negatively felt action or consequence.

> *Note, how both of these play well with two of the three core emotions that are succeptible to persuasion, according to Aristotle: hope, fear and empathy. As Aristotle defined in his groundbreaking work "Rhetoric", logos as one of three persuasive modes ethos, pathos and logos, involves "Emotional Appeal"–which concludes emotion sets in humans, that are most effective to target when attempting to persuade.*

Legitimate power is derived from a formally assigned position or role within a structured organization, that is based on established norms and values. Important for the general acceptance of this form of power is the initial acceptance of the structural composition, which inherits a formal acceptance of the predominant values and norms.

Referent power is based on loyalty within interpersonal relationships, that convey trust and attraction, often admiration. It can be described as charisma, which is not formally obtained, and has no formal status, that enables the individual to impose sanctions or grant benefits. The influence obtained by this power form is based on identification and a sense of inspirational appeal, mostly paired with a strong sense of trust that can exceed the one laid in a formal legitimate power type.

> *This form of power can become particularly dangerous when abused. When it seeks competition with a formally established, legitimate power, it can draw away obedience, and parallely make use of the succeptibility to manipulation, brought forth by undisputed loyalty. History has shown numerous examples, where abuse of referent power, particularly in conspiracy theories or pseudo-religious cults, culminated in violent acts that were explicitly aimed against other power types. While legitimate and referent power can coexist (see more timely actual phenomena like influencers, who earn money for paid promotion), it lies in their very nature, that referent power, through strong loyalty, can be weaponized. Conspiracy theorists make regular use of the established trust vested in them, to promote their views. Numerous historical examples have shown, that deliberate abuse of their followers' strong loyalty can reach points, where total disregard of any other authority escalated in physical violence and other criminal acts.*

Expert power is derived from superior knowledge or skills, that are widely respected and willingly accepted. The value of the power-holder's expertise and superior abilities in specialized areas is commonly accepted. This empowers the individual to obtain influence and directive decision-making capability.

Power, however, can also be observed through a lens other than base-oriented, external imposition or societal dynamics. It can be perceived as deeply embedded and rooted in societal structures and knowledge systems. Adding this specific layer of depth to the concept enables us to comprehend more hidden and substantial aspects of power, characterizing it as a mechanism of societal functionality. Foucault (1975) investigated the historical evolution of penal systems and their implications, particularly in educational institutions, prisons and medical practices. According to him, through subtle surveillance and control, a power form had been established, that helped to normalize behavior. While shifting from public spectacular executions to a regimented space of prison, the new form of power focused on surveilling and reforming an individual. The perceived sense of surveillance led to self-regulation in prisoners. Equally, educational institutions exert power through their rulebased regulation, exercised through timetables, classroom arrangements and examinations. Judgement and categorization encourage self-regulation and normalization of behavior in accordance with desired societal standards. In a similar sense, he claims, hospitals transformed patients into objects of scientific inquiry, by establishing a modern medical practice of observation, record-keeping and methods of examination and classification. This new form of regulating power, according to Foucault, helps creating obedient and more efficient (*i.e. productive*) individuals, through internalizing societal norms and staying in line with desired behavior.

In a similar fashion, the subtlety of power can be observed through a different lens than Foucault's disciplinary nature, that emphasizes embedding in societal norms. Subtle forms of power can also be explored by psychological and ideological aspects. According to Lukes (1974), there are three essential dimensions in which power operates in society. When he analyzed power in societies' structures, with a particular focus on how it shapes people's perceptions, preferences and beliefs, he examined political theories, as well as sociology and philosophy as foundations for the operating mechanisms of power in society. He challenged previous works, for example Dahl's, because he believed, that the threefold exercise of power was the one that most effectively explains societal Power Dynamics. His first dimension consists of observable conflicts. It is the most visible and perceptible form of power, that decides about who wins an argument, and how decisions are made. It is relatable and directly tangible in debates and decision-making. The second dimension is controlling an agenda. It is to be understood as the layering foundation of the first dimension, because controlling the agenda is foundational for the agenda to even set a selection of possible debates and subsequently, decisions. Scopelimitation as the second dimension is power, that is exercised less visibly than the first dimension, however, the exerted influence of control is larger. The entity that controls the agenda thereby indirectly exercises a large influence on final choices by limiting the scope of what is being publicly discussed. The third dimension describes the most subtle one, often remains entirely hidden and not noticed by the majority. It is the one that shapes dee-seated beliefs and desires, perceptions and convictions, beyond the grasp of the individual. Here, the influence is the largest, while at the same time visibility and realization is, most of the time, zero. This can happen through many different presets and gives the power-holder almost unlimited control.

> *Note, that the boundaries of the second and third dimension in Lukes' definition can be quite blurry. An effective agenda-controlling second dimension possesses traits of the third dimension in many cases, and vice versa. The effective control of agendas is a strong instrument in the limitation of knowledge, as well as the perception of what is important. An eventual decision-making and debate is a logical result of the agenda, that has been chosen in one or another way. While the most effective exercise of power is the one, that controls*

*an agenda and thus "flows" into a state of influ-
encing individual beliefs and perceptions. Since
each layer is embedded in the next, it is only logi-
cal, that an agenda is accepted, if an initial, subtly
exercised shaping power is already the insurance of
sufficient influence. The "masterpiece" of exertion
would thus be carrying out control in shaping desires, that are adopted in an approved agenda, with
subsequent visible display of argumentative power.
If the agenda's scope is already approved to be limited to "harmless" topics, the scope of the first dimension of power cannot harm the eminence of
the most subtle and hidden dimension. Master-
fully crafted, people would be made to think their
desires were fulfilled, unaware of the initial power
that controls their desires (and thus, the agenda),
and not the decisive debate.*

From the aforementioned theories, we may conclude, that
there are vast differences in perceiving power as lying within
an entity versus the one an individual possesses. Secondary
literature on those seminal theories often offers extensive views
and most of all, tailors them to contemporary contexts. Keltner (2016) investigated power through combinations of psychological research and historical examples, together with case
studies, which offers a unique exploration of everyday interactions, but likewise examples of historical leaders. Most interesting about his perspective is not only the acquisition and
possession of power, but also the demonstrations of its loss.
While often gained through socially intelligent behavior, quite
the opposite often took place, once these social traits were
abandoned in favor of selfserving action. On an individual
level, obtaining power often led to paradoxical behavior, because it could be shown, that on the individual-centric level,
the very personality traits, that once enabled intial obtain-
ment of power were soon forgotten, which caused the opposite.
Another individual-centered approach shows, that power it-

self is not inherently corruptive, but serves as a tool to amplify the very personality traits that are prevalent in the obtaining individual (Diamond, 2016). While self-awareness and empathy apparently leverage an ethical responsibility and the thoughtful exercise of power, it is equally used as a negative tool for negative intentions. This is not surprising, however, it could be clearly shown upon examples and case studies, that specifically observed non-state actors and tracked personal growth and traits. On a broader scale, moving from individual to entity, secondary literature suggests, that in modern international relations, numerous nonstate actors are apparently becoming increasingly influential (Baehr & Castermans-Holleman, 2010). While offering a macroscopic view of Power Dynamics, their work extends beyond state-centric perspectives and acknowledges the significant influence of other international actors, such as NGOs and other international organizations. This is a role, that had previously (i.e. traditionally) been a sole dominion of states. Those non-traditional actors rose to power over time, now equally shaping global policies and politics. In his collection of essays, Thomas Wartenberg (1992) was able to compile a range of analyses through different methodologies, in order to show, how power is conceptualized beyond the individual-centered view, and on a broader scale of socio-politics. It offers a large theoretical discourse around definitions and foundations of power, specifically seeking to include its dynamic and interrelated aspects.

2   MECHANICS OF POWER

2.1   Expressions: Authority, Influence, Control

In distinguishing expressive and interactive forms of power, we want to epitomize authority, influence and control as the expressive aspects, where power is projected from one entity or individual onto others. Generally speaking, authority is institutionalized power, that has some kind of recognition. Influence on the other hand, is often informal and rather persuasive. Control is the overt imposition of will, which can happen mainly through repression or directives and their subsequent enforcement. In the following subchapter, the three will be contrasted as to explain them in the broader context of mechanics of power.

Max Weber explored complex relationships between class, status and power in societal structures. He investigated the dynamics of those factors in order to provide foundational understanding for their mechanisms and distribution. Through examining different social systems, he found, that power and the overall organization of society are intertwined, especially through economy, politics and individual status. His early explorations helped make sense of social hierarchies in a nuanced framework (Weber, 1922). When Gerth & Mills (1946) translated a significant portion of Weber's works into the English language, his theories became more widespread, and furthermore, through careful editorial work, they were able to provide their compilation as a cornerstone in studies of contemporary sociology. The nature of authority, according to Weber, began to make sense in an entire discourse.

Especially in political power, the aspect of legitimacy is a key question. Legitimacy builds upon two cornerstones, which are a subjective sense of power acceptance in an individual and on the other hand a normative structure. In political discourse, they are of particular interest in contrasting democratic and nondemocratic systems (Beetham, 1991).

While each of the previously mentioned sources has their own descriptive aspects and their own interpretations of power, it is interesting to note, that many influential facets make for the different forms that it can shine through: force, manipulation, persuasion, authority and many more. They all have in common, that they are perceived to shape society in its core structures (Wrong, 1995). In the context of authority, Weber identifies it as a legitimate form of power, that has to be accepted by the individuals that are subjected to it. Beetham on the other hand, pays more attention to the normative structure, which shines a brighter light on the ethical and moral context, that make for the justification aspect. This especially differs from control and influence as we will explore, because those do not necessarily involve ethical considerations. Wrong's perspective supports that, because his work helps identify the authoritative aspect to be is grounded in societal norms and intrinsic structures.

Influence, as the second expressive form of power, is characterized by its subtlety and in contrast to authority, it is not formally asserted, or in need of formal approval or legitimacy. Influence, as previously stated, often operates through persuasive elements, thereby shaping behaviors and opinions, without the utilization of explicit commands or force (French & Raven, 1959; Cialdini, 2007). Influence does not impose or enforce rules and has no coercive aspect, because it rather stems from personal attributes. Cialdini, as an influential student of influence and persuasion, identified six principles of influence, namely: *reciprocity, commitment (and consis-*

tency), social proof, authority, liking, scarcity.

> *Note: While authority, from our perspective, cannot be a part of influence, I do not oppose Cialdini here. His described form of authority, in this particular regard, is different from the one I discussed, because authority, according to Cialdini's work, is rather the perceived authority, e.g. on account of expertise, rather than a formally established one.*

Influence as an expressive form of power can be derived from an individual's capability of communication, on account of skills, attitude and the ability to shape opinions (Kelman, 1958). It is important to understand, that it operates independently from other expressive power forms, and has its own way in contributing to Power Dynamics overall. In modern times, social media personalities and celebrities have their own power in influencing people, which often culminates in swaying public opinion, which can be an attractive source of income for some (Gladwell, 2000). The platforms used can vary, but the effective influence on masses of people that is wielded by public figures, is an own distinct form of personal power. The ability to resonate with a broad audience through charisma and connection, as previously highlighted in *Referent Power*, can be highly impactful.

An interesting short mention at this point is how profoundly influence can stand in contrast to other expressive power forms, because it is grounded in the resonance with personal values and beliefs, while authority and control can vastly conflict with those. As I will later discuss in more detail, the importance of autonomy in decision-making is a factor that can be substantially impaired when inner moral conflicts arise but the power of authority stands in contrast with own beliefs (Milgram, 1963). Since this was a fit within this chapter, I took the baseline of it and placed it here, but the details belong into the discussion about obedience and resistance in a later chapter.

Influence plays a crucial role in cultural contexts just as well, because often, the behavior, beliefs and opinions shaped in individuals are tightly connected to upbringing and peer contacts (Bandura, 1977), which translates to work environments. In the latter, authority is not present (*at least not in our current context*), and control is not primarily exerted in every leadership style, so it is at least not an omnipresent power factor, where there is put more emphasis on persuasion and inspiration in the workplace (Burt, 1992).

Control, as the third expressive power form, is characterized by a direct nature. It is commandoriented and thus set apart from authority and influence through its explicit enforcement of rules and directives. According to Bass (1990),

> *"Power over others depends on one's control of resources to give or deny and control of rewards and punishments to distribute. [...] in which members varied in the amount of control they could exercise over each other's avoidance of punishment. [...]"*

Control, according to Kipnis (1976), emphasizes measures that can include reward and punishment to ensure that outcomes and actions align with expectations or norms. This again underscores the commanding nature of control as a contrast to the consensus-building nature of influence. In organizational settings, bureaucratic structures are used as a means to clearly define rules and desired behavior, and likewise to ensure their obedience (Blau & Scott, 1962). This centralizes control as an expressive power form, rather than the decentralized form of influence, which is established on the grounds of personal charisma (Hollander, 1958).

While the effectiveness of control as a power exercising mechanism is seen in maintaining a desired order and thus, achieving a certain amount of predictability in particular contexts (Ouchi, 1979), it contrasts from authority in that it describes a direct and overt enforcement of compliance, while authority can exist without an active exercise of control. On the other hand, control somehow necessitates a form of authority in the first place, which shows in leadership: while a leader with an amount of authority, who lacks control mechanisms in organizational contexts, may still possess power on account of their legitimacy, but leadership attempting to exercise control while lacking authority may face resistance.

This is confirmed in Weber's views (1947), that show, how authority and control intersect in many ways, most importantly in their capacities to direct behavior and guide individual actions. However, Weber clarifies that implementation of control necessitates authority, because the capacity to exert power through control is grounded on the legitimacy, with which authority is justified, and thus accepted.

2.2 Interaction: Negotiation, Compliance, Resistance

One might wonder, why in the distinction between expressive power forms and power in interaction, negotiation is included here. As negotiation is often perceived as quite an opposite of what we have concluded so far, because it relies on mutual agreement and tends to use persuasive strategies rather than exerting superior assertive means from one party onto another. The reason is, that negotiation plays a huge role in the distribution of power weight between two parties. While the process of negotiation itself assumes some sort of a balanced distribution (*otherwise there would not be a need for the superior party to negotiate in the first place*), there are two main reasons, that negotiation is included here:

1. Often enough, the distribution of negotiation power is not equally balanced, hence there is a power imbalance between the parties (*think employer and employee*).

2. Power weightings can shift during a negotiation.

While the previously forms of social power were unite in their aspects of superiority of certain kinds, which made them *unilateral*, the nature of interactive Power Dynamics is *bilateral* or *multilateral*, i.e. they involve back-and-forth distribution of power aspects. That does not have to mean that there is not a superior involved, to remind you. But the pursuit of mutual agreement is in the foreground, rather than imposing a strict will (*and the capability of doing so, at least for the negotiated scope of action*).

Finding a middle ground of mutual acceptance is the nature of any negotiation scenario, which involves a collaborative approach to conflict resolution. The outcome of mutual gain is characterized by a more sustainable amount of satisfaction for the involves parties (Fisher et al., 2011). Although not always possible or achievable, the general narrative in a negotiation is the willingness to pursue a solution in a scenario of conflicting interests, that can lead to a perspective, that culminates in mutual benefit (Lewicki et al., 1985).

As Thompson (2009) found, negotiation requires skill and indeed a sort of strategy, which is why I initially mentioned, that Power Dynamics can change within a negotiated scenario. That is, certain parties can influence the way the negotiation evolves over the given timeframe, which makes for the original interactive aspect of it in the realm of Power Dynamics in general. Other than expressive power forms, the involvement of volatility in negotiation makes it an interesting subject of many socio-psychological studies. In need of skills like empathy and reading (*and responding to*) other parties' needs and interests, power in negotiation is mainly derived from sociological skill sets, that cannot be obtained through legitimacy or role status. Interpersonal understanding is the emphasis of negotiation power (Thompson, 2009). Negotiation is a way of moving away from the top-down approach of power to a rather democratic pursuit of effect and strategy. In fostering shared power and equal responsibility, it focuses on dialogue, compromise and collaboration (Kolb & Williams, 2001).

In one of my previous works, I have elaborated on compliance and resistance in the context of sociodynamics. When introduced, resistance was perceived as a phenomenon of individual psychology (Gross, 2023) and later extended to organizational contexts; I will form a synthesis thereof in the current context later on. As I have discussed, there are many different patterns in which both can show, however, in this book, I will elaborate on those, that play a key role in Power Dynamics, and particularly in the context of interactive power forms.

Compliance as an interactive power form is notably different from expressive forms like the aforementioned. It involves an interaction of reciprocal nature, so that one party conforms to the expectations of another. The important narrative is, that in contrast to negotiation, the own intrinsic desire may differ. That is, compliance can be practiced by one party without their own beliefs or opinions necessarily aligning with the request of the power holder. Individuals may comply, even if there is no acceptance of the directive (Asch, 1956), which reflects that there is an established relationship of imposing will. As Asch explains, factors contributing to compliance can be social norms, peer pressure or the desire to be accepted in a current circumstance. It does, however, not reflect an internal agreement. In contrast to influence, where an individual feels an internal alignment with the power holder, all action in congruency with the power holder's interests are done willingly.

> *Note: in organizational contexts, this can play a key role, because it makes a significant difference, if an individual only complies – for whatever reason – or is influenced, so that the obedience emerges from an internal desire to follow the lead. Especially, since the expressive power form of influence holds such sustainability, as I have mentioned, it might overpower compliance in certain situations.*

Given all that, compliance must still be contrasted against authority and control, since obeying organizational rules, and vice versa, the act of ensuring adherence to internal policies and procedures, does not necessarily require to impose authority. As mentioned, the pressure of fitting into a peer group can already be enough motivation to comply. Therefore, compliance is less rigid (Adler & Borys, 1996). As I have shown in my previous book, compliance is often firmly tied to peer pressure (Gross, 2023), and as I further referenced from Beattie (1963), the pressure imposed by informal groups (*i.e.* *peer-groups*) would often overpower the one imposed by an organization, which further supports my point here.

This sets the stage for understanding Milgram's seminal work on obedience, which is still famous in present day lectures in general psychology and sociology. Often simply referred to as the Milgram Experiment, it has gained popularity in explaining how the aforementioned pressure can cause a form of compliance, that does not only not align with personal beliefs and moral codes, it can even be diametrically opposed. Milgram's experiment illustrated the extent to which individuals were willing to comply with the demands of figures that were perceived as superior. As shocking as it was, the willingness to comply went as far as to inflict (perceived) harm on others (Milgram, 1963). The experiment involved a staged scenario, where there were subjects that were administered to test "other subjects" (that were really confederates of the lab) upon their memory. The subjects were instructed to distribute electric shocks to the individuals they believed to be the actual subjects, in cases they "failed to complete the task". Interestingly, what started out as mild electric shocks would increase to more and more severe shocks, up to the point where the believed subjects were in visible physical pain. The subjects were further instructed to inflict the shocks upon false answers in what was perceived by by them to be utter disregard of the pain and noticeable discomfort of the "staged" subjects. With a few exceptions that uttered concern and eventually disobeyed to further administer electric shocks, the subjects would comply and, opposing their actual inner moral codes, inflict shocks onto the subjects of which they knew they would cause severe physical pain and potentially even danger.

Note: a discussion that I had with my professor back in the day comes to my mind, when I speak about the experiment. Something that, according to my own research, has been discussed rather rarely was not only the willingness by the subjects to comply with the orders of what they perceived as authority figures. Interestingly enough, they were willing to administer physical harm to persons they did not know, on behalf of persons they did not know, either. In my opinion, there lies another interesting aspect of the experiment: the fact, that the subjects – except for those ones, who started seriously questioning the instructors and eventually disobeyed their orders could, at the time, not know what the consequences of their compliance would be. In fact, it was not only obedience that showed through compliance with the ordered distribution of electrical shocks, it was also the trust for their professionalism and correct estimation of the potential danger the believed-to-be probands would be put in. While the actual subjects of the study were fully aware, that they would administer the shocks themselves, they had no way of knowing, what the consequences might be. I also find it interesting, that the perception of authority could be established so quickly. In the same way that the experiment was able to show the extent of compliance, it was interesting to see how easily it could originally be established, to a point where an informed individual would take actions in full awareness, on behalf of a total stranger, that they had to believe might be suitable to put someone they did not knew, either, in physical danger.

Milgram and future referencing works provided a crucial transition of the understanding of social pressure and -conformity, which has sustainably shaped the discourse of Power Dynamics to the present day. Milgram himself referenced to it again almost ten years later, when he talked about the *"Perils of Obedience"* (1974). Another eight years later, the implications of the experiment were re-investigated in order to draw conclusions for the contemporary understanding of the long-term impact on compliance paradigm (Blass, 1981). It is important to mention, that from our perspective for this book, the experiment has implications for more than only compliance, because the cornerstones of it concerned authority and influence as well.

Considering Power Dynamics, another famous study complements that by Milgram and has gained no less attention, being commonly known as the *Stanford Experiment*, which was conducted in 1971. While having a different setting, it delved deep into the social structures of power and individual adaptation to assigned roles. The experiment simulated a prison environment at the beginning of which volunteers were randomly assigned roles of either guards or inmates. The aim of this setup was to study the psychological effects of these assigned roles on the subjects' displayed behavior. The experiment gained tremendous popularity mainly through the infamous abuse of power that the guards quickly exhibited. While all participants adopted their assigned roles rather fast, guards quickly began to display authoritarian behavior, while inmates began to behave rather submissive. The experiment notably escalated within only a few days, which caused an unplanned abortion way before the actual maturity of two planned weeks. While the duration fell short of expectations, the learning curve certainly did not. If you will, the expected role adaptations were only condensed, in a way that even after less than a week, the extreme nature of behavior on account of the (*randomly!*) assigned roles showed to overpower moral codes and previous neutrality.

Sadly, the extent to which the experiment harmed the subjects, was one of the reasons it would later be profoundly criticized and sparked a subsequent debate on ethics in psychological research. However, I believe that at the time, the outcome of the experiment was at least as much of a surprise to the researchers as it had been to the participants. In the realm of the debate, sometimes, the generalizability for a real world application was questioned, as the participants had originally known the artificial nature of the settings. *The question about methodological limitations however, in my opinion, is not quite restrictive of the impact, on the contrary: given the fact, that all subjects were fully aware of their roles and that they could equally have been assigned the opposite role makes for a much more impactful statement in regard of the quick overpowering effect that the settings had onto their inner moral code.*

Zimbardo himself reacted to the countless works that have been grounded on his experiment with another work of 2007, titled *"The Lucifer Effect: Understanding How Good People Turn Evil"*. Some other influential works, that center around the findings of the experiment, confirm its impact in bringing it into virtually any scientific discussion on compliance in social hierarchy dynamics, which shows its enduring relevance (Maslach, 1996). It serves as an example showcase in many debates on ethics in research (Loughan et al., 2013) and most importantly, it is one of the most seminal works on abuse of power, moral degradation and the effects of perceived power over peer individuals. Thus, it is of great importance in discussions about Power Dynamics in sociological contexts (Haney & Banks, 1975).

As I mentioned before, quite the opposite of compliance is the factor of resistance. Although resistance does not necessarily lead to eventual noncompliance, it describes an act of defying the demands of others. While resistance can occur in various forms, they all share the common trait of standing in stark contrast to compliance. The forms can reach from passive non-compliance to overt and active opposition. Resistance involves a conscious and deliberate decision to push back against requests, orders or expectations, regardless of the potential reason.

According to Piderit (2000), in organizational contexts, resistance is often seen when employees oppose certain changes in internal policies or management decisions. Reasons for resistance can be equally manifold, ranging from the internal desire to retain autonomy to a certain extent, or to pursue personal interests rather than aligning with superior decisions or peer pressure. Often, a subjectively felt injustice can be either the reason or at least contribute to resistance, even when the perceived injustice is on behalf of others. This is specifically the case when resistance is observed in oppressive systems (*e.g. political*) and the choice is made to stand up against the oppressor(s) (Sharp, 1973). It is especially driven by the belief, that compliance in some sense perpetuates the status that is felt as oppressive.

While characterized by an oppositional nature, the breeding grounds for resistance must be defined by some sort of motivation. It can stand in contrast with fear or repression, especially when it comes to political contexts, which then often equals an internal battle of morale and fear. While power upholds the oppression against individuals, the empowerment of resistant forces is often driven by a certain spark which ignites a *"too much is too much"-attitude*. According to Piderit, the very intention carried by resistance is mainly the desire to bring forth social change, while highlighting the injustices that originally sparked the resistant movement.

While political and social injustices are socially explainable in their striving for moving towards an equilibrium, there are other forms, where it can work as a rather irrational force, that carries destructive power. In destructive scenarios, resistance can do quite the opposite, in functioning as an inhibitor of positive change, and rather causing conflict and social disruption (Hollander & Einwohner, 2004).

> *The reason, why I characterize some forms and contexts of resistance as "irrational" is rooted in the perspective, that in those cases where I do, the resistance is, in fact, counterproductive to the resisting force itself. Sometimes, in organizational contexts, resistance is grounded on an irrational fear of change and the subsequent necessity for personal adaptation. It can come down to mere laziness in some individuals, that a certain form*

of passive resistance is formed against implementation against novel ideas, technologies or structures. I have experienced this phenomenon in various contexts, whereof many showed a certain strong prevalence across German public administration authorities and government-administered educational facilities. To me, it often seemed as if the attitude against positive innovation was somewhat inherited from previous generations and would then be passed on. I have not failed to mention it in various symposiums that I sat in, or during conferences, yet with little to no acknowledgement, which was little surprising given the fact that we're talking about resistance in the first place. However, irrationality was the feeling that always sat with me when I observed this sort of selfprotective behavior. The extent of protectionism in defense of "traditional" methods, attitudes and general administration of tasks would more than once go as far as negating any contribution to possible positive change. Even to the point, where the resisting force could plainly see the beneficial potential, and to the point where it got blatantly ridiculous. Motivations were often driven by a fear of losing a customary right, status, missing out, general distrust, lack of knowledge of facts and unwillingness to just about any sort of personal development and adaptation. Which, I want to add, are all reasons one would most certainly not like to admit, and therefore justifications for resistance would get outright absurd.

Here, a psychological factor comes into play – *reactance*. According to Brehm & Brehm (1981) it occurs as a response to a perceived threat to individual autonomy. The interesting aspect is, that it is solely based on the perception of a threat, with no necessity for a substantiated threat. In a scenario, where an individual feels the chain of decisions might lead up to their freedom of choice being constrained by authority or control, there often arises the tendency to resist, which is an act in order to assert independence. This can happen regardless of the true nature or intention of the would-be implementation of change. Tyler (2006) finds, that this sort of behavior can stem from a lack of inclusiveness in the overall process of decision-making, which appears to be an indicator for such perceptions, even if they are untrue.

3 EMOTIONAL INTELLIGENCE IN POWER DYNAMICS

3.1 Fundamentals: Self-Awareness, Self-Regulation as Social Skills

The development of first concepts of Emotional Intelligence (EQ) is relatively young when studied in the context of Power Dynamics. It first gained notable attention through introduction of a monitoring model presented by Salovey & Mayer (1990), that had been designed to serve as a guide for one's own emotions and actions. This is the transition from external power manifestations to internal emotional processes that shape and influence them individually. Although their work did not directly draw conclusions from, or put an emphasis on Power Dynamics, they have a number of intersections that contribute to today's understanding of leadership strategies and interpersonal relationships that are of utter importance, not at least in language proficiency.

Emotional Intelligence is the ability to monitor one's own emotions and get them aligned with a certain context, in the realm of Self-Awareness. According to Salovey & Mayer (1990), this is a contributing factor to better interpersonal relationships, as one's recognition of emotions reflect in more balanced and rational decisions and eventually, actions. Those findings had somewhat a groundbreaking character to them, because in the socio-psychological discourse, the consideration of emotions within the realm of *intelligence* had not been common at the time. Our transition to Power Dynamics sits at the point, where Daniel Goleman adopted the terminology and concept when he argued, that Emotional Intelligence was just about as important as the then-traditional intelligence concepts of logic and so on (Goleman, 1995). His line of arguments was, that Emotional Intelligence with all its facets was an utterly critical factor for success in life, because it had substantial impact on all levels of interpersonal relationships – including one's professional environment. Together with fellow researchers Boyatzis and McKee, Goleman advocated for the recognition of Emotional Intelligence as a key factor in overall assessment of intelligence, since he had been able to demonstrate how deep-reaching selfawareness and the management of one's own emotions affected professional areas like leadership styles, conflict resolution and strategies in negotiation, compliance and resistance (Goleman et al., 2002).

And *here* is our transition: All the aforementioned have vast implications for Power Dynamics, since they are key components of power expression and interaction and exert a considerable influence on interpersonal relations. Moreover, they directly intersect with communication and are therefore building a myriad of sub-factors that are important to consider when delving into language proficiency and communication science.

Self-awareness as a key component of EQ, describes the ability to understand how one's actions and emotions impact other individuals. It is not limited to perceiving, but being *actively aware* of the consequent impact and causality. *In that regard, I would define it as follows: It means the ability to comprehend the relationship between cause and effect on an emotional level.*[1]

In organizational contexts, it has been found, that leaders

---

[1]Self-Awareness shares common traits with the concept of *Metacognition*. I have published a work on the history of the development of theories on Metacognition, that explores how it evolved in psychology over time (Gross, 2023).

with a higher EQ understand and manage their own emotions better, as well as they can better react upon those of their subordinates. In conclusion, this leads to better outcomes in Sociodynamics (Goleman, 1998). According to Salovey & Mayer (1990), individuals with higher EQ are generally better equipped to make informed choices on the grounds of their empathetic understanding. *This is not surprising, as in a scenario where Person A is little aware of Person B's current or general emotional structure, it will, upon regular sociocultural interaction, only be a matter of time until a conflict arises, that puts Person A before a major challenge. Conflict resolution with a low EQ will become distinctly harder and consist of many more challenges, due to the little amount of emotional reflection abilities. Besides from that, for Person B, this situation can be frustrating because of the feeling of emotional neglect.*

On the other hand, the person with a higher EQ does not only have a certain amount of awareness of their own emotional state and how it affects others, the ability to anticipate others' reactions is something, that puts someone in advantage in communicative settings. The timely sense for a reaction upon own actions lets someone adjust their approach in the next step. This transitions in more effective communication, accordingly (Bar-On, 2006).

As I have discussed in the predecessor of this book, effectiveness is the ultimate goal in communication and its nature defines, that we opt for mutual understanding (Gross, 2023). I elaborated on this in particular regard of the *Cooperative Principle* introduced by Grice (1975), who put an emphasis on a number of maxims that were the essential building blocks of utterances in order to achieve effectiveness in communication. He also asserted, that human communication is intrinsically wired to *cooperate*, which means Speaker A has an internal, natural desire for Speaker B to make sense of their words, and thus, effectiveness can be learned and trained. In the same way, the achievement of higher effectiveness in communicative scenarios can be a product of higher EQ, because naturally, tailoring one's own approach to sensed emotional states of the counterpart makes for a valuable aid in strategic communication. According to a work by Brown & Treviño (2006), in management skills, ethics in leadership are becoming increasingly essential, much of which is grounded in self-awareness as a core factor of ethical governance.

As an extension to self-awareness, *self-regulation* adds an additional layer of behavioral control to the understanding of an individual's emotions. While self-awareness remains at a cognitive level, self-regulation extends to both levels, cognitive and behavioral (BarOn, 2006; Pekaar et al., 2018; Martinez-Pons, 2000). It involves an initial identification and understanding of one's emotions, and in the following, an active intervention to control and adapt an emotional response to a certain situational context.

In the broader context of Power Dynamics and Emotional Intelligence, self-regulation plays a key role, because power and its expressions and interactions can elicit strong emotional reactions in an individual. That is, the regulation of subsequent actions in oneself is a key ability for staying in control of the entire situation. The reason why self-regulation is at the basis of behavioral science and accordingly, investigations of Power Dynamics, is, that the management of stress typically involves personal *and* work-related factors, that will often clash in work environments. It does not only have important effects on management and leadership performance, but, regarding the twofold nature, is also a key component of personal health and mental well-being (Slaski & Cartwright, 2002). Since complex Power Dynamics can add to the difficulty of managing emotions, appropriately responding to them is crucial for the maintenance of productivity and interpersonal relations.

> *We all know scenarios, where a person is put under a lot of stress and at a certain point is no more in control of their emotions. Interpersonal conflicts arise, naturally, because the person ap-*

proaches their inner so-called "breaking point", at which the pressure becomes too high and something in reach serves as a valve to let off pressure. Unfortunately, this rarely happens in a situation that is well-suited, because typically that requires either good chance or a proper management of "holding it in" for long enough. The typical scenario however, that most of us know from experience of everyday life, is, that the person will have a go at someone who is not to blame, or will burn out or exert any other destructive behavior. More often than not, it could have been prevented through a proper self-assessment at an earlier point in time. We often do not experience social pressure as an immediate force that hits us in an unforseeable manner. Stress and social distress rather builds up inside all of us, and we should address them before they cause damage.

These of my annotations are supported by Goleman (1995), who asserted, that the ability to control (or redirect) disruptive impulses and individual moods characterizes the attribute of thinking before acting which is the exact behavior, that in the aforementioned scenario has become impossible. In that regard, not only the own mental well-being is affected, but also intersocial relations, often even sustainably, if the outburst was severe enough. Self-regulation as a practice in the realm of Power Dynamics and EQ, on the other hand, contributes to quality social relationships, exhibiting so-called prosocial tendencies (Lopes et al., 2005). It can be regarded as the opposite of reacting impulsively, which is a behavior that especially in crises, can add substantially to the severity of the situation. As a contrast, retaining a calm manner, even in high-pressure situations, is a key skill for leadership, and in social scenarios in general, as it puts at the forefront the process of balancing out emotional arousal with cognitive regulation processes (Blair & Diamond, 2007) – a trait that requires rationality and thus allows for a much more accurate assessment of the situation in question.

3.2 EQ in the Exercise of Power: Leadership, Empathy and Motivation

Leadership in a classic, historical sense, can be traced back to eras as early as ancient civilizations, such as Mesopotamia and Egypt. For all we know about those, there were concepts of authority that were held at the time by pharaohs and other ancient rulers (Bass & Bass, 2008). The modern concepts of leadership however, that primarily shaped today's understanding of leadership concepts, began to form during the Industrial Revolution. Scholars like Max Weber introduced ideas of leaders as individuals with exceptional qualities (Weber, 1947). It was also the time when leadership as an academic field of study emerged and began to gain attention in the social sciences. Notable researchers like Kurt Lewin (1939) began to explore the concept as a behavioral study. Likewise, one of the most influential works on social power, that has been extensively referenced in this book, is French & Raven's 1959 work, that observes leadership and its relationships with social power and hierarchies.

Within our framework of Power Dynamics, and more particularly through the lens of EQ, leadership emphasizes the ability of the power holder to recognize and understand their own emotions, as well as those of their subordinates. Paired with the recognition and understanding is a distinct ability to manage those emotions effectively, which makes for outstanding communication skills (George, 2000). For a leader, it is of particular interest to inspire others, rather than exert mere authority (Prati et al., 2003), which aligns with our previous clarification, that modern forms of effective management have successively moved away from top-down systems that do not acknowledge needs and desires of subordinates. This reflects in many studies on leadership, that have emphasized the human traits a leader should possess in order to inspire and motivate (Palmer et al., 2001), which requires emotional acknowledgement and connection with a team, further establishing a relationship characterized by trust. This all culminates in a positive team- and work environment and fosters a sense of democracy and participation, rather than imposing strict top-down orders and controlling their obedience.

> Note, how at an earlier point, I explained, how referent power and influence are sustainably strong forces in Power Dynamics that are specifically characterized by the high willingness to align with the power holding individual's goals and opinions. It is a logical conclusion, that the employment of a relationship of trust and identification, translates to a strong leadership. Vice versa, the establishment of a highly authoritative relationship may inherit strong power, but it lacks the social sense of participation and is often bound to function as an impediment in the implementation of ideas and progress, due to a much higher readiness to resist. It is important to understand, how these social forces and the intrinsic emotional interweavings work together and influence each other.

While ancient, or traditional, leadership models were not especially ineffective, they put their emphasis on the coercive aspect of Power Dynamics and had little regard for emotional depth. In modern times, perceptions of effective leaders have changed to a picture, that has not completely abandoned the authoritative traits, but seeks to blend them with an additional layer of emotional understanding to leverage the powers of shaping opinions and actions. This additional layer is characterized by a dimension of empathetic understanding, as a means to practice guidance through inspiration and participation, rather than strict enforcement and control (Côté et al., 2010). The extent of participation certainly has its limitations at the very point where the assertive domain of the power holder begins. Modern leadership does not disregard or even discard hierarchy, it lays its focus on a more appealing form of practice.

> *For a long time, those two distinct perceptions had been believed to oppose each other. While in strict top-down exercise of power, any sort of demo-cratic inclusion was perceived as a threat, that put authority in danger, moving away from author-ity and control would have been a weakness that endangered the hierarchical structure. Nowadays, perceptions about that have drastically changed. An emotionally intelligent leader is no more per-ceived as a weak spot, on the contrary. Through all of the scientific works we are assessing here, it be-comes clear, that the archaic perception of imple-mentation of EQ in leadership being diametrically opposed to hierarchy is indeed false. Quite the op-posite is true: though it has certainly taken some courage, it could be found, that the modern under-standing of empathetic guidance creates an even stronger form of obedience through influence. As I have shown, this has numerous advantages, par-ticularly when it comes to quick adaptations and effectiveness.*

Since the general narrative in leadership studies has begun to incorporate ethical questions and putting a strong em-phasis on team cohesion, emotional support and understand-ing, fostering a positive work environment with employment-wellbeing (Dearborn, 2002), it could be proven, that the nav-igation of the emotional landscape in organizations, as an addition to the structural one, leads to more effective and adaptational processes (Martin, 2016) and eventually, more success (Dearborn, 2002).

The concept of empathy has a rich and early history and has evolved through social sciences and psychology until the present day, eventually translating into modern leadership and organizational theories, that we observe in the context of Power Dynamics and Emotional Intelligence. Adam Smith, as early as 1759, grounded empathy's ancient philosophical roots in his work *Theory of Moral Sentiments*, in discussing *sympathy* as an individual's ability to understand others' feelings and share them accordingly. In the psychological discourse of the early 20th century, the term *empathy* was discussed by figures like Titchener (1909), who described it as the ability to understand others' experiences. In its evolution through social sciences and psychology, empathy became a critical topic in psychological education, because it grew as one of the key concepts in therapeutic environments (Rogers, 1957). In our context of Power Dynamics, Daniel Goleman (1995, 1998, 2006) highlighted its role in Emotional Intelligence, underscoring its importance for modern leadership theories and effectiveness in interpersonal relationships.

Contrasted with the initially introduced expressive forms of power, authority and control, empathy stands in stark opposition. In its ability to reflect others' emotions, it greatly influences how power is exercised and likewise, perceived (*by both parties*). As mentioned before, environments, that are subjectively perceived as inclusive and understanding in nature, foster a sense of belonging and cooperation, rather than obligation and rule enforcement. Through employing empathy, leaders become more aware of cause and effect in an emotional sense, which gives them the ability to grow and adapt and which reflects in how they build trust and participation with their followers (Kellett et al., 2006).

I would not like to be repetitive, so I will focus on one particular contrast, before moving on in the context. Empathy as a cooperative trait in power exercise and leadership is especially interesting when compared with the most extreme forms in Power Dynamics, such as oppression. While it is a concept that puts its emphasis on understanding and acknowledgement of others' emotions, in order to act upon that understanding, oppression not seldomly exerts the total opposite. In oppressive scenarios, the attitude of the power holder towards the emotions and mental wellbeing of others can range from indifferent to downright hostile. This reflects in cognitive and behavioral levels, as empathy is also not only a cognitive aspect, but includes appropriately responding to others' emotions (Hoffmann, 2001).

The cooperative traits of empathy lead up to another pivotal aspect of Power Dynamics and leadership in that context: motivation as a force to inspiration and as an aspect of Emotional Intelligence. In contrast with top-down authoritative power, which leaves little space for personal development and cooperation, motivation is an essential aspect of leading emotionally intelligently. While there are certain motivational aspects of authoritative power exercise, they are distinct from motivation in a context of EQ. The difference is, that within the former, motivational forces are *external*, e.g. coercive or rewarding, while motivation in the context of Emotional Intelligence is *internal*, because it involves sparking an intrinsic drive for inspiration and engagement. The distinction can be perceived as the extent of voluntariness in each. While coercive power is clear to spark fear to an extent, rewarding power is characterized by hope. Motivation, in our context, on the other hand, stems from a certain ability of the power holder to access the emotional level of others.

Note: in my opinion, this is a phenomenon that is worth discussing in the context of general developmental psychology, or a humanistic perspective. When we perceive the distinction between authority and empathetic motivation as externally and internally motivational factors, and their driving forces, we can hypothesize, that external motivation in this case, we stick with coercive and rewarding power – is caused by a stimulus that engages inner desires for physiological and safety needs. Physiological, blatantly, is the absence of pain (as the most basic and extreme exertion of power is the infliction of physical harm as a form of pun-

ishment). Safety, here in a sense of securement, translates to securing basic, life-ensuring assets, in modern age accessed through money, which in this context comes down to rewarding power. Here, external motivation through coercive and rewarding power ends. As we discuss, we grow aware, that both of those form the two bottom parts of Maslow's (1943) hierarchy of needs. We may perceive the limited access of these externally motivational forces to the entire self of an individual, as they come down to the bottom two factors. Now, as we have acknowledged, the internally motivational form is characterized by sparking a sense of inner engagement and inspiration, because it leaves the exact room for development that I described, in a way that appreciates own input and often, creativity. This, in contrast to the former, translates to higher levels in the hierarchy of needs, leading up to the ultimate potential for satisfaction, through embarking on self-actualization.

The fact, that external motivation has limited access to higher levels of need-hierarchies makes it obvious, in my opinion, that the correlation between developmental psychology and humanism on the one hand, and Power Dynamics on the other hand, has implications for the perspectives we should take in this context. Since the form of motivation I am introducing in this chapter, defined by Emotional Intelligence, includes and builds upon the satisfaction of physiological and safety needs, it must, according to this humanistic perspective, contribute to higherlevel human satisfaction, as internal motivation.

Ryan & Deci (2000) found, that motivation within emotionally intelligent leadership is particularly characterized by fostering a sense of shared purpose among followers, that is the basis of higher enthusiasm and individual commitment. Moreover, in a sense of ethical leadership, the leader functions as an example of promoted values, that transitions onto their followers, creating an environment characterized by fairness, respect for each other (*including the leader*) and altruism (Brown & Mitchell, 2010).

Altogether, the concept of fostering intrinsic motivation stands in a stark contrast to traditional and more ancient leadership systems in top-down manner, that had little regard for individual development, emotional well-being and understanding emotions. While externally imposed motivation (*even rewarding*) can lead to a lack of personal and emotional investment over time, internally motivating factors spark the own sense of appreciation, development and foster engagement. The feeling of shared puspose leads to altruism, that puts the shared values over individual ones (Kark & Van Dijk, 2007).

4 STRUCTURES AND EFFECT IN HIERARCHIES

4.1 Layers, Roles and Communication Flow

The historical perspective of *hierarchy*, that has its roots ancient Greek philosophy, blends into the overarching topic of Power Dynamics, as it forms the original foundation of the very structures that we are observing and discussing. With ancient thinker Plato, who, in his seminal work *The Republic* (380 BCE), attempted a first means to classify the ideal form of society into classes based on their abilities, laid the first cornerstone of our understanding of hierarchical conceptualizations. His most popular student, Aristotle, adopted some of his thoughts on social order and extended on socio-political theories in his seminal work *Politics* (~350BCE), wherein he explored ideas of social hierarchies and especially the role of citizens in a citystate (*polity*), that provides comprehensive insights in power organization and authority concepts.

Layers in hierarchies refer to different levels within a hierarchical structure, of which each has its own distinct attributes, such as roles, reponsibilities and own Power Dynamics. These layers have a significant impact onto *how* power is exercised and perceived. Across each layer in a hierarchical composition, the nature of power can change. Mintzberg (1983) found, that in a division into three distinct layers, for management environments, the top layer typically possesses decision-making authority, while within the middle management, there are more collaborative and influence-based positions. The lower layers are typically execution-focused. In organizational psychology, the layers of hierarchies are often brought in context with managing complexity and making complex systems comprehensible through decomposability (Wu, 2013).[1]

Hierarchical structures help streamline decisionmaking in organizational contexts in reducing the complex organizational structure through hierarchical layers (Boyer, 2004), which is often perceived as a pyramid figure, with more general information at the top and more elaborated information towards the bottom (Martins & Villringer, 2018). Interestingly, the concept of hierarchical layers has been found to translate to everyday contexts as well, therefore extending from organizational contexts to structures like social networks and the internet (Goussevskaia et al., 2007). Those layers influence not only efficiency in routing tasks, but have implications for career paths and general behavioral tendencies of employees, or generally, individuals that deal with them (Tåg et al., 2016).

In understanding Power Dynamics, it is essential to familiarize oneself with the concept of hierarchical layers, because they have strong intersections with Emotional Intelligence. It is crucial for a leader, to understand the broader impact of management decisions across other layers, which includes bottom layers just as well, because the organization is an entity, that only functions through the inclusion of functionality in each distinct layer. As Mayer et al. (2008) found, managing their own emotions is a critically skill for leaders, because understanding the emotional responses of others within the organization affects the whole firm.

---

[1] *Decomposability, in this context, means breaking down complexities into smaller, better comprehensible and manageable pieces, as a means to make everyday tasks more organized and less overwhelming.*

Note: It is critical for upper layers in a hierarchical structure to anticipate the scope and outreach of their decisions not only in their own layer, which is an ability that real life shows us, is not always selfevident. A case example in April 2017 gained international attention, when United Express, a domestic branch of United Airlines, enforced a very ill-conceived decision made by management at the time. They decided to have four paying customers removed from a flight on the Chicago O'Hare site, destined to Louisville. The reason was to make room for four of United's staff deadheading the flight in order to be carried to the destination for work purposes on the following day. Three of the four randomly chosen passengers to leave the plane complied, whereas one, a pulmonologist, who claimed to have patients to treat at the destination on the next day, refused. In the following, he was forcefully removed from the flight by security officers, under display of what was perceived as exaggerated physical force, that led to the passsenger's injury and foremost, unprecedented public outrage. Due to the enclosed space in the aircraft, other passengers were put at immediate exposition and chose to film the incident and share it on global social media. The extent of criticism was horrendous, leading up to the US president issuing a statement on the case. United top management issued a statement in defense of the practice, which fuelled the outrage even more, eventually culminating in substantial stock price decrease for United. The case was settled financially in what was termed "amicable" for the passenger, however the damage in reputation was done, regardless of a later issued apology by United Airlines.

This case example serves as an impactful reminder of how emotionally intelligent leadership does not only have implications on the own layer in hierarchy, but must acknowledge the entire scope of management actions, that can often have global outreach through the public keeping a careful eye on the actions of top layer's actions. Since the lower layers in hierarchical structures are the ones, that most often directly interact with customers, the Emotional Intelligence in a top layer should acknowledge the scope and extent to which their decisions have an influence on those layers, too. In the displayed example of United Airlines, that was clearly not the case. The execution of daily operations may have become substantially more difficult for these employees, certainly being under especially scrutiny and being exposed to harsh criticism for their organizations policies, despite having no direct influence on them. The example shows drastically, that informed decision-making in top layers must always be responsive of the realities in bottom layers. Jordan & Trotz (2004) stated, that the experiences of those at the operational level should inform the decisions that are made above them. This transitions well into our general Emotional Intelligence investigation, as Huy (1999, p. 342) understands:

> "It is difficult to imagine an internal capability that is more tracid and idiosyncratic than the emotional energy of loyal members. Emotional capability taps the organization's emotional energy, which represents one of the most poorly understood and underexploited internal capabilities. For too long, emotional energy bas been treated as irrational or nefarious to sound organizing. This article exposes an alternative view: far from being an impediment to learning and change, emotional capability theory predicts, that well-channeled emotional dynamics can lead to the realization of radical, or second-order, change. Unattended, suppressed, or disdained emotional energy can frus-

trate the careers of many change agents. For firms faced with an increasingly dynamic environment, emotional energy represents a largely unexploited, yet ready, resource. Well tapped, it will enable organizations to realize strategic stretch."

In conclusion, Emotional Intelligence encompasses accurate reasoning of emotions, and the usage of emotions and knowledge about emotions to enable and enhance according thought and action (Mayer & Salovey), specifically with leaders' EQ affecting satisfaction and even extra-role behavior of lower-layer subordinates (Wong & Law, 2002).

The term roles in the same context, refers to specific functions or positions within each layer. That is, roles describe which organizational position an individual has within the overall hierarchy. According to Huy (1999), they are different from layers, as they focus on the responsibilities of an individual, and accordingly, their behaviors, rather than the stratum of hierarchy. With each position in a hierarchical order, there are associated particular duties – hence, each role inherits its own set of Power Dynamics and therewith, its own requirements for specific Emotional Intelligence (George, 2000). While the dissimilarities in layers and roles are primarily in their focus and scope (Mintzberg, 1983), they do also share common traits, because they both touch on navigation and management of power relations (Jordan & Troth, 2004), which include one's own and those of others. It is important to understand, that the layer in a hierarchically structured entity can include several distinct roles, each with their own power structure. Sunindijo (2012) found, that each position in an organization comes with unique focuses, responsibilities and challenges, which makes them hard to generalize.

That is, you cannot simply determine, that top- or middle management have their typical role or status, with common responsibilities; an important observation in regard of hierarchy theory. While it

is a fact, that the distribution of power within or-
ganizations follows some general rules, as we have
established, it is not merely generalized, how they
work dynamically, since this can vastly differ from
entity to entity, or even from layer to layer.

In contrast to some ancient perceptions about how power works from the top down and has little to no implications on bottom layers, according to Druskat & Wolff (2001), it does not make a difference for the effective management of power and communication, which layer is concerned. The ability to empathize and manage relationships effectively is crucial for effective and successful exercise of power on all levels. Transitioning to our next sub-topic, communication flow within entities, Vigoda-Gadot & Meisler (2010) state, that EQ, across all levels and roles, facilitates this flow by ensuring, that all interactions are conducted with an understanding of and respect for the emotional underpinnings and individual implications. This is further supported by Singh & Dubey's 2015 work on the intertwined nature of layers and roles in hierarchies, that demand effective emotional management across all levels of an entity in order to ensure successful organizational functioning.

In dissecting *communication flow* in the context of layers and roles in hierarchies, it is important to understand, that the term is not limited to the transfer of information from one entity to another. The how is much more of interest: how is information conveyed, how is it received and interpreted, and how does this flow work its way across different layers and roles within an organization? One of the vital attributes we have to include in this question is the question of accuracy, that defines the extent to which visions, goals, orders and expectations from higher layers are communicated effectively down to lower layers, and to which extent can they be understood as to exercise the necessary steps (George, 2000). In that regard, EQ plays a significant role in enhancing communication flow, because as we already established earlier, leaders with a high EQ express their ideas clearly and effectively and with a high regard for their subordinates' emotional perceptions. It is a vital component of communication, to convey insights about realities back and forth in a way of mutual comprehension (Men, 2014; George, 2000).

> *This is not a one-way street. It is equally important, that on-ground realities are communicated upwards equally effectively, because they do not only form the foundation for subsequent decision-making, they are otherwise likely overlooked. We do currently have numerous examples in contemporary politics and governance, where this way of communication flow is lacking acknowledgement. In authorities, I have often perceived, how there were new guidelines established, that were vastly counterproductive and in some cases, even impossible to implement (at least in the required time-frame). Many of those cases were grounded on insufficient communication flow in the direction towards higher layers, because the necessary forum was not given to employees. The results are imaginable: as we previously learned, the resistance, especially the passive form, is a means to disobey newly imposed rules and new guidelines, that can often threaten existing frameworks. While I mentioned, that there are indeed irrational examples, where resistance is grounded on mere attitude of opposition, without a rational reason, this which we observe here, is very different: in a hierarchy system, that does not effectively work their communication flow in both directions, it is only a matter of time, until top layers distribute their impossible-toimplement requirements to bottom layers, and the result is almost always resistance. Not only is this resistance grounded on the impossibility of the underlying requirement, it is an*

*emotional resistance just as well: employees feel
vastly undervalued if there is such little regard for
their needs, or the subjective feeling of a lack of
interest because of the limited knowledge about on-
ground realities. In the context of Power Dynamics, this can lead to the perception of a ruling elite
class with centralized power, that imposes their expectations on lower-level individuals with total disregard for their reality. The result is dysfunction,
in one way or another.*

Sy et al. (2006) support that which I said, since they
state, communication flow helps balancing out Power Dynamics among different layers and roles in hierarchies. A functioning communication flow in both directions allows for a more
participative and inclusive environment within the entity, because it takes away the scenario where decisions are unilat-
erally imposed from the top down. Shaping novel directions
through inclusive and collaborative environments ensures the
support (*physically and ideologically*) of bottom layers. As
we can now sufficiently derive from previous assessments, this
makes for a much larger amount of overall felt appreciation,
value and eventually satisfaction – while otherwise, the opposite is the case. Exchange of information is also crucial in
both ways, because when changes are made, it is crucial to
have assessments and feedbacks, which are important in every layer. Inputs from all levels ensure smooth transitions,
better implementation, more refinement and after all, better
acceptance (Schneider et al., 2013). In regard of EQ, it exchanges emotions just as well as the original information, if
conducted efficiently, which again makes for the foundation of
respectful and empathetic collaboration across different layers and roles within the hierarchical structure (Wolff, 2013;
Xie et al., 2021).

I want to add, that from my own experience, especially in situations where changes or implementations are timely due, a lack of proper commu-

nication flow can threaten the entire action, even leading up to its total failure. This has been observed in many cases, especially where feedback-loops were not taken seriously enough. Prominent examples from the last 20 years are more than enough, e.g. Nokia and Volkswagen. While those are largescale examples, there are many smaller ones, where communication flow at least slows down timely pressing implementations. Paired with a general attitude of resistance, which is the deadliest cocktail in the scenario, the possibilities to react upon scenarios in a timely efficient manner, are almost zero.

4.2 Strategies and Barriers in Leadership and Hierarchy: A Case Study Example on Upward and Downward Internal and External Communication Flow

As we established in the previous chapter, the essence of communication flow in hierarchies embodies the processes of delivery, reception and interpretation of information, which transcends its mere exchange. In emotionally intelligent leadership, and with regard to our previously asserted composition of roles and layers within hierarchical structures, it is crucial that information be conveyed effectively and comprehensively, and it has been shown, that it has to function bidirectionally. As to explore this in more rigor, I would like to incorporate a case study on this very subject, that has undertaken a large-scale investigation in a large entity, exploring the communication flow in context of the organizational hierarchy.

In this chapter, you will see, that my previous assertions about the directions and dynamics in communication flow translate well into real life scenarios and that it can be empirically shown, how knowledge of social science and psychology has its implications for mathematically measurable Power Dynamics. The depth of analysis of the presented case study is scientifically robust and likewise, practically applicable, whereas at some points difficult to grasp. I will try and convey the essential information in an understandable manner.

The case study, titled *"Communication network dynamics in a large organizational hierarchy"* (Josephs et al., 2022) sparked my interest in the literature search immediately, and as I found, it served my chapter so well, that I decided to integrate it as a means to support my previous assertions in more detail.

In a large-scale investigation of email communication among about 200,000 employees, there were email counts by employees and their according roles within the internal hierarchy investigated. The study investigates degree distributions within the email network, eventually revealing a skewed distribution with a small number of subjects having a high amount of communication. The study further assesses the power-law distribution of total degrees, with an estimated exponent, indicating scale-free network properties.

The study introduces the *EI-index* as a metric to quantify external vs. internal communication and proposes other metrics to calculate email reciprocation upon specific traits of the internal hierarchy composition. A few of the essential measures are positioned below.

Krackhardt and Stern (1988) argue that successful organizations respond better to crises when there are links between different teams, hypothesizing that organizations with a positive EI-index will respond effectively to crises. The EI-index for team i and the organization EI-index are given as

$$\text{EI-index}(i) = \frac{EL(i) - IL(i)}{EL(i) + IL(i)} \quad \text{and} \quad \text{EI-index} = \frac{\sum_i (EL(i) - IL(i))}{\sum_i (EL(i) + IL(i))} .$$

respectively, where $EL(i)$ and $IL(i)$ are the number of external (between teams) and internal (within team) links, respectively, for team i:

$$EL(i) = \sum_{\substack{u \in \text{team } i \\ v \notin \text{team } i}} \mathbb{1}(A_{uv} + A_{vu} > 0) \quad \text{and} \quad IL(i) = \sum_{u,v \in \text{team } i} \mathbb{1}(A_{uv} + A_{vu} > 0) .$$

Explanation of the EI-index; measure of the balance between external and internal links within teams. A higher EI-index means, that a team is more externally focused.

Next, we investigate the dynamics of emails that are sent by employees compared to those that are received. Link reciprocity for directed networks has been well studied in both binary (Garlaschelli and Loffredo, 2004) and weighted settings (Squartini et al., 2013). The reciprocity of our email network is $r = 0.31$ (SD $= 0.01$) without the weights and $r = 0.40$ (SD $= 0.14$) with the weights. However, we are interested in reciprocity at the individual node level. For this, we propose two measures of node-level reciprocity. First, we measure the proportion of sent emails that are part of reciprocated communications, which we refer to as *sent reciprocation*. That is, the proportion of all email relationships in which u sent at least one email to v among all recipients v who ever sent an email to u. We similarly measure the proportion of received emails, or *received reciprocation*. For any individual u, these are defined as

$$SR(u) = \frac{\sum_v \mathbb{1}(A_{uv} > 0)\mathbb{1}(A_{vu} > 0)}{\sum_v \mathbb{1}(A_{uv} > 0)} \quad \text{and} \quad RR(u) = \frac{\sum_v \mathbb{1}(A_{vu} > 0)\mathbb{1}(A_{uv} > 0)}{\sum_v \mathbb{1}(A_{vu} > 0)} .$$

respectively. Figure [4] shows the difference of these proportions as a function of the employee's level, which we recall is the number of steps below the CEO in the organization, relative to the depth of that employee's team. This normalization ensures that employees that are at the bottom of their team's hierarchy are grouped together no matter how deep each team is. We see that employees higher in the organization send emails that are reciprocated more often than they reciprocate emails that they receive.

Sent and Received Reciprocation; indices to measure the proportion of SR and RR that are part of reciprocated communication. This overview provides insight and understanding of the reciprocation balance at any level.

For every individual u in team r, the *hierarchical position* (Hoeva et al., 2017) is

$$HP(u) = \frac{\sum_{v \in r} D_{uv}}{n_r - 1}$$

where D_{uv} is the *hierarchical difference* between u and $v \in$ team r.

$$D_{uv} = \begin{cases} +1 & \text{if } u \text{ is higher than } v \text{ in the hierarchy} \\ 0 & \text{if } u \text{ is on the same level as } v \text{ in the hierarchy} \\ -1 & \text{if } u \text{ is lower than } v \text{ in the hierarchy} \end{cases}$$

Inspired by this differencing, we define *sent position* and *received position* for individual u as

$$SP(u) = \frac{\sum_{v \in r} I(A_{uv} > 0) \cdot D_{uv}}{\sum_v I(A_{uv} > 0)} \quad \text{and} \quad RP(u) = \frac{\sum_{v \in r} I(A_{vu} > 0) \cdot D_{uv}}{\sum_v I(A_{vu} > 0)}$$

Here, the former are brought in context with the internal hierarchical structure. HP(u) represents the hierarchical position of an individual within its team. D_{uv} is the hierarchical difference between individuals u and v.

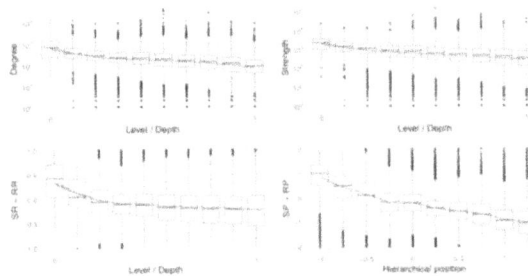

Figure 4. Measures of team-level email communication and reciprocity by organizational position. (Top) Total degree and strength in the entire email network by relative position in the organization. (Bottom) Left: Difference in the proportions SR and RR by relative position in the organization hierarchy. Right: Difference in the signed proportions SP and RP by HP. In all of the plots, we bin position into 10 equal groupings and we show the box plot within each bin along with a smoothed curve (blue) of the individual (non-binned) data.

We define three notions of reporting distance as a function of these path length quantities: *reporting distance*, *signed reporting distance*, and *directed reporting distance*. Respectively, these distances between u and v are defined as

$$RD(u, v) = n^{up}(u, v) + n^{down}(u, v) ,$$
$$SRD(u, v) = n^{up}(u, v) - n^{down}(u, v) ,$$
$$DRD(u, v) = RD(u, v) \cdot \mathrm{sgn}(SRD(u, v)) .$$

Graphical plot of degree of the mail network by relative position in the hierarchical structure, and below, description of the Reporting Distance.

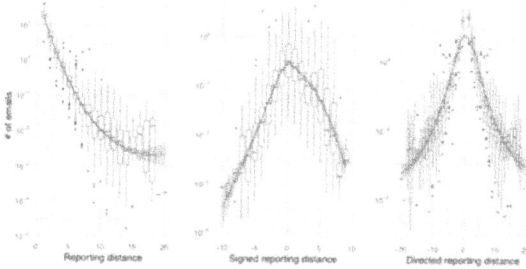

Figure 5: Pairwise reporting distances in the organizational tree and the average number of emails among all pairs in that reporting distance. Reporting distances are computed within each team and the box plots summarize the results across all of the teams. The individual team plots are shown in Appendix Figure A.5.

This shows that communication increases exponentially by local proximity to others, similar to the the global clustering in Figure 2.

Does the frequency of communication between employees depend on their relative ranks in the organizational hierarchy? To assess whether the right and center plots of Figure 5 are symmetric about zero, we perform two permutation tests. Let $S_k = \{(u, v) : \text{DRD}(u, v) = k\}$. We construct a test statistic as

$$t(A) = \sum_{k=1}^{k_{max}} \left(\frac{1}{|S_k|} \sum_{(u,v) \in S_k} A_{uv} - \frac{1}{|S_{-k}|} \sum_{(u,v) \in S_{-k}} A_{uv} \right)^2 .$$

where $k_{max} = \max_{u,v} \text{DRD}(u, v)$. We obtain a null distribution by randomly permuting the number of emails exchanged among pairs whose reporting distances are the same. That is, by permuting the rows/columns of A within the sets $S_k \cup S_{-k}$ for $k = 1, \ldots, k_{max}$. For each replicate, we obtain a new email network A from which we can compute $t(A)$. By design, the relationship between the DRD in the organizational tree and communication in A is symmetric around 0 under this permutation.

Graphical plot of the Reporting Distance, and subsequent calculation of permutation tests. Target was to find out, whether the frequency of email exchanges was dependent on hierarchical positions relative to each other. The findings showed imbalances between DRD, which indicates there was either more top-down or bottom-up communication flow (in communicative pairs), but in terms of SRD (which is a more holistic perspective in this regard, investigating the totality of communication flow direction-wise), the flow appeared to be more balanced.

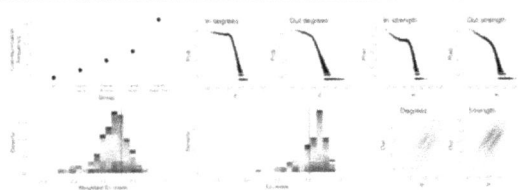

Figure 3: (Top) Left: Frequency of communication within different groups in the organization. Middle: In-degree and out-degree distributions. Right: In-strength and out-strength distributions. (Bottom) Right: Bivariate (in vs out) degree and strength distributions. Middle: Distribution of EI-index across (and colored by) teams, where the vertical line represents the entire organization's EI-index. (Left): Distribution of weighted EI-index across teams.

Graphical plot of the EI-indices, visualizing internal and external flow with low EI score for high internal and high EI score for high external bound flow. It is visible, that in the plot of the weighted EI-index, there is a higher cluster towards the right (positive side) across the different teams, which means that there is a higher outbound flow relative to the inbound. On the top right, in strength and out strength represent the total volume of connections, while in and out degrees visualize the number of different connections to a single node. The downward slopes of in- and out degrees and strength on the log-log scale represent a decreasing probability distribution, the higher the number of degrees and the higher the strength. This aligns with the general assumption of "network hubs": only few nodes have a very high number of degrees and strength, while the vast majority of nodes has a much lower number.

For an understanding of these imbalances, the distinction and asymmetries in DRD and SRD illustrate the complexities in dynamics of hierarchical communication. The asymmetry in DRD specifically, highlights that there is a prevalence of bias in direction of communication flow, while more symmetry in SRD shows the importance of bidirectional communication, as mentioned earlier. The statistical rigor of this study demonstrates, that the conclusion I made before, are empirically grounded and can be proven in real-life entities.

In conclusion, Josephs et al.'s study demonstrates clearly, how communication is distributed in a hierarchical organization. The skewed distribution of communication, which can be interpreted through the lens of EQ and Power Dynamics, might suggest, that those with a higher EQ might be more effectively communicating, resulting in a higher number of interactions. Judging from the suggested EI-index, an understanding conclusion of managing team dynamics could suggest, that a higher index indicates more responsiveness to external stimuli, which is generally associated with high collective EQ. While the study found asymmetrically distributed communication patterns, the direction and flow of communication can often provide insight into the power structure, reflected in either a stronger bottom-up or top-down prevalence. These numbers, reflecting hierarchical context, can inform us about where power originates from and where decision-making predominantly lies within the organization. This, after all, allows us to draw significant conclusions about how Power Dynamics shape communication patterns.

Own conclusive thoughts

The provided study, to me, serves as a significant empirical quantitative backbone to the previous, qualitatively assessed, understanding of effective communication in multidimensional environments. It must be clear, reciprocal and likewise, emotionally intelligent. As it has been shown, effective communication flow is a determinant of efficiency and health within a hierarchical organization: information does not only travel along a vertical axis, but functions as a complex web across the entire structure. While doing that, the flow of communication does not solely serve logistical purposes, but also strategic ones, as it can either empower or inhibit effective leadership and information exchange. While the study proves skewed distributions in communication flow, it mirrors critical roles of certain individuals within the structure. While those are not necessarily power holders in our context, they much rather highlight the human element of Emotional Intelligence, exhibited through influence of some sorts. Being central communicators, those individuals ensure team agility and intern cohesion. Furthermore, the nuanced interplay in reciprocity underscores the distribution in influence even more, as there is not a dynamic equilibrium, but rather a centered gravity of those, who probably display a large amount of Emotional Intelligence and thus, exhibit particular gravitative forms of power. Those do not always have to align with assigned authority within the hierarchical system. In an ideal scenario, communication flows would be entirely balanced out in the up-streams and down-streams, allowing for seamless ground-level experience to be transmitted to higher layers within the hierarchy, and likewise, providing a downward dissemination of directives and visions. When communicative flows are disrupted, or become one-directional instead of bidirectional, it can constrain leadership and culminates in a lack of information at bottom layers. The results can be as I have elaborated in other chapters: misunderstanding, resistance, or even misconceptions. Given all the assessed information, it can be concluded, that multidirectional flows in communication are absolutely crucial in order to maintain an engaged workforce, while factors like Emotional Intelligence highly influence Power Dynamics in the context of hierarchically structured communication.

5 POWER IMBALANCES AND EMPATHETIC APPROACHES TO POWER RELATIONS

5.1 Imbalance Recognition, Strategies and Language Use

Power imbalance, as the term suggests, refers to unequal distribution of power among individuals or groups, measured in a specific scope. It often leads to dominance by one of the parties. With a pioneering work, Blau (1964) analyzed social life on a broader scale, in order to derive complex social structures from more obvious ones, among them imbalances in social power. Two decades later, Knights & Willmott (1989) explored power and subjectivity in sociological contexts. Furthermore, in their 2002 work *Writing organizational analysis into* Foucault, especially drawing upon Foucault's seminal works, where they explored *panoptic organization*, driven by surveillance and constant scrutiny in organizational structures, leading to vast imbalances in power. At this point, we are coming back to different forms of power, that can work in a rather active or passive way, depending on the target, for example in actively hindering issues from emerging (Bachrach & Baratz, 1962). In 2010, Lovett described an idea power balance as the absence or reduction of dependency and a minimized amount of domination. This, according to Lovett, has implications for social order and relationships, due to the re-

53

duction of arbitrary imbalances in power distribution.

In this chapter, however, I would first like to address the psychological effects of power imbalances and how to address them, as a means to align the subtopic with our context of Power Dynamics and EQ. Therefore, it is necessary to briefly explore the psychological insights on power imbalance, before addressing their origins and recognition, in order to discuss strategies (*specifically in the context of language use and - proficiency*).

In exploring how power discrepancies affect individuals on a psychological level, it is important to observe, what extrinsic power display causes on an intrinsic level in an individual. A subjectively felt imbalance leads to diminished self-worth and often creates feelings of helplessness and insecurity (Keltner et al., 2003). The results are emotional distress, up to exhaustion and deep-sitting frustration. A phenomenon termed *learned helplessness* describes the emotional state, where an individual in a lower power position inherits the feeling of worthlessness and lack of control over their own situation (Seligman, 1972). This does not always relate to power imbalance, though, but through a perceived overpowerment, there is a process of getting accustomed to reduced inner motivation and thus a lack of engagement, that can cause mental distress and affect mental health sustainably.

From the perspective of the power holder, however, there are also significant effects of power imbalance on the psychological level. The subjective effects can be overstatement and an inflated perception of self-worth, practically mirroring the opposite perspective, which often corresponds with a lack of empathy for subordinates (Fast et al., 2012). As you understand, such personality traits reflect a low EQ, which, in turn, does not promise sustainable success in a high-power position. The concept of EQ however, can help mitigate the negative effects of power imbalances quite reliably (Brackett et al., 2011).

Recognition of power imbalances is not always easy, as we have already discussed, that power does not always correspond to assigned roles or obvious traits. In rather subtle power forms, the recognition of imbalances is therefore much more difficult. In organizational contexts, imbalances can exist across different departments, or between individuals (Eagly & Carli, 2007).

> *Note: it is important to see this in a broader context of hierarchical structures, because if we determine a structure from layers of power and across different roles, those do indeed not always have to reflect the actual distribution of power. It is not only possible, but rather even usual, that within the same layers in a hierarchy, there still exist imbalances in actually-held power.*

However, timely recognition of those imbalances is vital for the successful management of relationships within an entity (Mayer et al., 2018; Knudson-Martin et al., 2015), because only then, management can avoid power clusters at unwanted places, and also manage emotions effectively. From a perspective of Emotional Intelligence, awareness for power relations is highly needed, because, according to Brass & Burkhardt (1993), empathetic approaches are only effective if they incorporate a focus on understanding experiences and perspectives of those who hold less powerful positions. This is a confirmation of the psychological effects, that we established a well-managing, emotionally intelligent leader prompts in subordinates: the feeling of appreciation, being taken seriously and of interest. This involves active listening [part of another book of this series] and the valuing of input of others, leading to inclusion in decision-making and democratic environments, which are essential markers for positive and supportive organizational and working cultures (Lupton, 1995; Decety, 2015). The recognition of power imbalances in an organization can lead to proactive measures like mentorship programs, changes in policies and specific initiatives to empower underrepresented groups. This eventually creates more equitable environments in working culture and has shown to increase productivity (Ely et al., 2011; HartnerTiefenthaler, 2020).

The following page provides an overview of timely actual example studies, that show the truth of the aforementioned assertions:

- **Blanck et al., 2020:** *Legal profession*
Workplace accommodations for lawyers with disabilities and those who identified themselves as LGBTQ+ have shown positive impacts, while requests were higher among women.

- **Hur, 2020:** *Public sector*
Positive influences through inclusive practices for LGBTQ+, overall increase in job satisfaction and commitment to the organization. Practices include fairness-, cooperation- and empowerment-oriented measures.

- **Lindsay et al., 2022:** *Healthcare professions*
The creation of more inclusive workplace environments for professionals with disabilities showed crucial for mental well-being and also career development, while enhancing diversity in the workforce.

- **van Laar et al., 2019:** *General workforce*
LGBTQ+ individuals, ethnic and other minorities who face stigma in the workplace, show a significant need for the promotion of equality and inclusion.

- **Tang et al., 2021:** *Financial services*
Adressing challenges faced by lesbian and bisexual individuals in the financial service industry in Hong Kong leads to more productive outcomes.

- **Perales et al., 2021:** *Inclusive language*
Trans-affirming language in Australia contributes to inclusion of diverse gender employees and their wellbeing.

5.2 Connection and Conflict Resolution

Individuals in lower layers of a hierarchical structure are more prone to being exposed to the negative aspects of power imbalances and thus are at a higher risk of feeling undervalued and less appreciated. Due to differing perspectives and interests, lower power positions can easily convey a feeling of being overlooked (Deutsch, 2006). In this context, resolving conflicts that arise on account of imbalances is a critical aspect of emotionally intelligent leadership. Connection refers to the ability of a leader to provide a sense of understanding, irrespective of the other's position in the hierarchy. Empathy is one of the core skills to conflict resolution in the face of power imbalances, because often, the underlying Power Dynamics have led or at least contributed to the conflict in the first place (Ury et al., 1988). Conflict resolution, in this regard, has a sense of empowerment and lending a voice to those, who are less powerful, as a means to acknowledge their perspective. This does not mean to compromise the rights or grants of others, but moving towards a resolution that respects the needs and concerns of every involved party at an equal level (Goleman, 1998).

> *While it is mainly not the origin of an imbalance, that a specific party in a middle layer benefits from excessive power on expense of lower layers, it is mainly the unattended and improperly addressed concerns of certain layers or even individuals, that cause subjectively felt injustice. This is the main aspect of an emotionally intelligent conflict resolution. It does not necessarily mean to redistribute power concentrations, but rather to lift underrepresented individuals or groups to a level of equality. This again, requires the priorly discussed bidirectional communication flow, because only if addressed properly by both sides, there is a fruitful discourse. Communicating effectively and emotionally intelligent is thus not only a necessity*

for higher layers in a hierarchy, but should equally guide the bottom-up discussion.

Typical examples for proper, emotionally intelligent approaches to conflict resolution in the bottom-up scenario involve:

1. **Active Feedback Channels** – established feedback mechanisms, such as suggestion boxes, meetings or proposal of solutions to conflicts.

2. **Initiatives for Open Dialogue** – open discussion forums, that enable everyone equally to express their views directly to higher layers. This enables short communication ways and promotes understanding.

3. **Internal Networks** – in demonstrating understanding of the social power and networks within an entity, communication effect can be leveraged.

4. **Intelligent Advocacy** – framing problems in a persuasive way, that outlines shared and common goals.

5. **Solution-oriented Communication** – demonstration of investment beyond personal or immediate interests shows commitment to the greater good and sustainable way of thinking.

All those elements intertwine into a comprehensive framework to conflict resolution in an organizational and interpersonal context. Communication proficiency involves understanding subtle hints in Power Dynamics, that are often left unspoken, hence I advocate for such topics to be included in the greater frame of language proficiency in higher education. Reading Power Dynamics involves the ability to *"read the room"*, understand the unspoken cues in social scenarios, and adapt one's own messages accordingly. It does not necessarily require an initial position of high power, to communicate effectively and achieve communicative success. That is, articulation of ideas and feedback, keeping conversation concise and tailored to context are skills that can be improved through practice. According to Watzlawick et al., the how is the key component: in order to be heard and respected by higher levels of power in an organization, it all comes down to the skillful crafting or messages and how they are proficiently conveyed in the right situation. Sociopsychological intelligence extends beyond the concept of Emotional Intelligence, because it also includes the understanding of group dynamics and organizational culture. Social norms play a key role in organizations, and only an individual who is capable of navigating them effectively, will achieve success in communicating ideas and needs. Through a deep understanding of how power is distributed and how it works dynamically, individuals are enabled to walk their own path through the maze of hierarchies and cultivate an own recognition of cues and the overall functionality of Power Dynamics. After all, deeper understanding of social realities provides a much better approach to timely effective conflict resolution, that holds a sustainable potential. Educating this is key to wellbeing.

6 EMPOWERING EDUCATIONAL ENVIRONMENTS: CLASSROOM DYNAMICS, CURRICULUM DESIGN

In every classroom and lecturing hall, or more generally speaking, every educational situation, there are Power Dynamics. As we have treated organizational contexts, as well as political and social ones quite extensively, and since this work is a resource for higher education, it is paramount, that we have a brief look into classroom dynamics as well. As curriculum design and well-managed classroom dynamics enhance empowerment, engagement from either side and effective learning and studying (Hattie, 2009), this is a chapter that is equally important for students as it is for teachers and professors. The relationships between students and teaching staff and also among students themselves are a foundational component of the overall learning experience. Only if they work effectively, with established boundaries, and a comforting and inclusive feeling, the outcome is as desired (Cornelius-White, 2007; Freiberg, 1999). When it comes to curriculum design, which is a scientific discipline for itself, contemporary educational theories suggest, that it becomes more relatable, engaging and applicable for students, if they are able to reflect and draw upon reallife experiences (Wiggins & McTighe, 2005), which is understandable since from a psychological perspective, we all tend to compare and connect new knowledge with an already existing knowledge base (Bruner, 1973).

It is a natural process in our brain, that translates to so-called "situative learning", that suggests, that learning in a specific context we can relate to opens up perspectives we have previously taken and that strengthens our application of new knowledge through a deeper understanding (Lave & Wenger, 1991). From a neuroscientific point of view, neural connectivity explains, how we connect education to real-life experiences through neural plasticity: it is the process of strengthening existing neural connections (Draganski et al., 2004). According to Paller & Wagner (2002), it is also a process, that has profound implications on more effective memory consolidation, because relating education and new knowledge to existing knowledge and experiences in real-life situations engages our emotions.

With that foundation, classroom dynamics should involve active learning strategies and collaborative projects, along open communication channels, that establish an atmosphere of inclusion and participation. Students should always be encouraged to share their thoughts and opinions, instead of overpowering them. Project-based learning is not only engaging, but fosters creativity, which again opens up channels for more discussion and discourse among peers, but also between student and teacher. Diverse learning needs must be addressed with equality, because it ensures that all students have equal opportunities (Tomlinson, 2001; Heacox, 2002). Elias et al. (1997) and Durlak et al. (2011) suggest, that educational environments are crucial for building interpersonal relationships, just as they are for academic purposes. The early exposition with peers, where foundations for Emotional Intelligence are laid, must be perceived as a preparation for future workplace scenarios.

In the context of Power Dynamics, the establishment of clear boundaries between students and teachers is a crucial aspect for both sides. Clear boundaries set by teaching staff help in creating a supportive and safe environment for students (Brophy, 2006), which fosters a productive learning and working atmosphere. This does not mean imposing overly restrictive rule sets onto students, because that would cause an unwanted imbalance, that hinders communication and affects the student-teacher relationship negatively (Rogers & Freiberg, 1994). It is rather the maintenance of discipline and rules that contribute to a positive classroom culture, encouraging students' engagement and willingness to participate in the learning process actively.

In peer relationships, Power Dynamics often show in competitive scenarios. While it is natural, that they occur, it is vital for educators to acknowledge, that competition among students can be both beneficial and detrimental (Johnson & Johnson, 1989). While a healthy form of competition fosters the natural interest and engagement, and a particular motivation to strive for excellence, competition can also become excessive and lead to stress and anxiety. It is essential for educational personnel to lead and guide through such scenarios, while maintaining a positive attitude among students (Kohn, 1992). It requires a careful consideration, in which scenarios competition can be beneficial for the overall classroom culture. Especially in terms of inclusive education, it is essential to treat competition very considerate as to respect those that lack certain abilities and avoid any sort of discrimination. Furthermore, excess competition can lead to an exaggerated focus on winning on expense of the greater purpose of learning and social engagement. Including healthy forms of competition in the right scenarios is a demanding task for educators, because it has to be wellimplemented in the peer dynamics alongside the promotion of mutual support and while keeping an eye on the educational task at hand (Slavin, 1995). According to Gillies (2003) competition should not be focused on merely outperforming others, because it contradicts the idea of collaborative achievement. It is rather beneficial if each student feels valued for their own contribution to a greater whole.

7 CONCLUSION

As a conclusive chapter, these lines are meant to recap the knowledge and to synthesize the different aspects Power Dynamics in regard of the context of communication psychology in higher education.

Tracing the evolution of Power Dynamics from its historical emergence in ancient social philosophy, it could be shown how in evolving societies, power has been perceived differently throughout different eras of time. This journey could provide us with a deeper understanding of how power, once perceived primarily as an aspect and a tool of dominance and control, could evolve into a much more nuanced concept with many societal and interpersonal facets. Through exploring the mechanisms of power, divided into essential forms like expressive and interactive, a more complex picture emerged, giving insight into the subtle nature of power exercise and illustrating the complex and interwoven character and interplay of power forms and how they deeply affect relationships of groups and individuals.

As a central element to this discourse, Emotional Intelligence could be dissected into various nuanced parts, and made comprehensible as an interconnected concept of self-awareness, which shares various traits with the psychological theories on metacognition, selfregulation as one of the key elements effective communication, that adds a behavioral dimension to the cognitive realm of self-awareness, and also the important implications on leadership. While empathetic communication is one of the key abilities in effective modern

65

leadership, it had long been dominated by the sentiment of total authority and control. While methods of surveillance and scrutiny were certainly functional elements of exercising power, it has been established, that empathetic leadership leads to more sustainable, long-term success, with much more satisfaction on both sides. Achieved through emotionally intelligent communication flow, organizational culture has evolved substantially over the course of years, decades, even centuries.

These insights led us to the investigation of hierarchies and how they can be dissected into their very components, depending on the perspective; while hierarchical structures could be decomposed into several layers, it was also important, to get a fundamental understanding of roles inside hierarchies and how they influence and are influenced by power distribution. The examination and explanation of a large-scale case study helped understand the real-world application of these layers, in shedding light on the communication flow within a large company. In extrapolating those findings on upward and downward internal and external communication flow, we were able to form conclusions on general communication patterns in hierarchically structured organization and it was made clear, that only a bidirectional functionality ensures long-term successful exchange of ideas, concerns and information. Especially in delving into the empathetic aspect of communication, it could be clearly demonstrated through a large number of referenced examples and studies, that modern leadership necessitates a well-rounded communicational approach in order to show value and appreciation to subordinates and that organizational communication is a key determinant of its health and function. Only if both sides work together in effective communication, there can be fostered an enriching, motivating, inclusive and appreciative environment in an organization, that, without neglecting hierarchical positions, provides a fair ground for everyone to evolve and feel safe and eventually satisfied.

In synthesizing these aspects into modern education, it

could be shown, that educational environments are essentially no different from other social atmospheres, benefitting from sound knowledge about sociopsychological facts and communicational expertise. While a certain amount of competitive behavior can have beneficial aspects for education in general, it obliges to the educator to balance out attitudes of students and implementing clearly communicated boundaries in order to facilitate a productive environment for everybody. Especially in modern inclusive education, it is important, that communication be emotionally intelligent as a means to avoid and proactively fight discrimination.

After all, psychological knowledge is a very important asset to communication and all linguistic proficiency is worth nothing if poorly executed.

ACKNOWLEDGEMENTS

Ich möchte an dieser Stelle einer ganzen Reihe an Menschen danken, die in den letzten Jahren, und auch unmittelbar während des Pozesses dieser Buchreihe indirekt und direkt dazu beigetragen haben, dass ich in der Lage war, dieses Werk entstehen zu lassen. Darüber hinaus nutze ich diese Zeilen, um generellen Dank auszusprechen für die Unterstützung von vielen Seiten, die nicht nur dieses Buch, sondern die Plattform von I.C.A.P.E. und deren Wachstum gefördert haben – dies hat den eigentlichen Grundstein dafür gelegt, dass ich mich entschieden habe, dieses Werk überhaupt erst zu verfassen.

Mein größter Dank gebührt meinen **Eltern**, Theresia und Wolfram Gross, die mich mein ganzes Leben in all meinen Entscheidungen voll und ganz unterstützt haben und nach wie vor mit Rat und Tat an meiner Seite stehen. Ich konnte mich immer voll und ganz auf euch verlassen und ihr seid immer da. Euch ist nicht nur dieses bisher umfangreichste Volume gewidmet, sondern die gesamte Reihe. Danke für alles. Ich danke meinem Kollegen und Freund **Dr. Dr. Vesselin Petkov**, der als Vorsitzender des Minkowski Institus mit dem angeschlossenen akademischen Verlag, der Minkowski Institute Press, die Herausgabe dieses Werks ermöglicht hat, und dessen Kritik des Buchs mich in meiner Arbeit sehr ermutigt und motiviert hat. Es ist mir eine große Ehre. Mein Freund und und Forschungspartner **André Michaud** verdient meine höchste Anerkennung für seine Beiträge zu meinem Wissen in Neurolinguistik und für seine unermüdliche Arbeit für unser *International Council of Academics for Progressive Education*, insbesondere für den wertvollen Input zu unserer akade-

mischen Struktur. Yassine Zerrouki, Vice Chair von
I.C.A.P.E., dir danke ich für fachliche, organisatorische und
emotione Unterstützung, mein Freund. Ich danke **Dr. Dr.
P.K. Paul**, für weitreichende akademische Unterstützung und
Zusammenarbeit, die Einladungen zu akademischen Konferen-
zen und Herstellung von wichtigen Kontakten in der akademischen Welt. Im Rahmen meiner Funktion als der Vorsitzende
von I.C.A.P.E. danke ich außerdem **Dr. A. Hamood** und
Dr. Sławomira Kołsut für interessante Beiträge, Koop-
erationen und Forschungsbeteiligung, auch in unserem bereits anstehenden kommenden Projekt zur postnatalen Myelin-
bildung in den Brodmann Arealen des Gehirns. Ich freue
mich darauf. Ich danke dem gesamten Team vom Campus
der Macromedia University Frankfurt am Main, für die sehr
gute Organisation und schöne Zusammenarbeit in diversen
akademischen Bereichen an der Fakultät für Kultur, Medien
und Psychologie. Desweiteren danke ich **Dr. Christian
Metz, Sven Kischewski, Anabell Westrich** und **Nicole
Sauter** als meine besten und sehr motivierten Schüler. Mein
Dank für beratende Worte geht außerdem an **Prof. Dr.
Dr. Philipp Plugmann**, der sich die Zeit genommen hat,
mich persönlich in seiner Freizeit in meiner Arbeit hier mit
seinem umfangreichen Wissen und seiner Erfahrung zu un-
terstützen. Ich bin **Dr. Christian Schütz** dankbar für viele
unterstützende Gespräche, insbesondere im Rahmen der gele-
gentlichen mentalen Talfahrten. Ich danke meinem gesamten
Team im **Advisory Board** von I.C.A.P.E. für die Arbeit
und das, was wir gemeinsam erreicht haben. Ich möchte an
dieser Stelle auch **Prof. Dr. Jaromir Konecny** erwähnen,
von dem ich viel über Artificial Intelligence gelernt habe, und
der regelmäßig sinnstiftende Beiträge zur Community leistet,
von denen ich bereits mehrfach profitieren durfte, und der
auch im persönlichen Kontakt ein sehr lieber Kollege ist. Ich
danke außerdem Prof. Dr. Sheron Fraser-Burgess für die
Veröffentlichung des I.C.A.P.E. Newsletters *"Ethische Fragestel-
lungen in der modernen Bildung"* im letzten Jahr.
Natürlich danke ich **allen** anderen **Kollegen, Studenten**

und **Freunden** ebenso sehr, dafür, dass ich das tun darf, was mir Freude macht und für die Wertschätzung und das Voranbringen meiner Arbeit.

BIBLIOGRAPHY

ACTFL. (2012). ACTFL proficiency guidelines.

Adler, P. S., & Borys, B. (1996). Two types of bureaucracy: Enabling and coercive. Administrative Science Quarterly, 41(1), 61-89.

Aristotle. (350BCE). "Politics." (B. Jowett, Trans.)

Asch, S. E. (1956). Studies of independence and conformity: A minority of one against a unanimous majority. Psychological Monographs: General and Applied, 70(9), 1-70.

Bachrach, P., & Baratz, M. (1962). Two Faces of Power. American Political Science Review.

Baehr, P. R., & Castermans-Holleman, M. (Eds.). (2010). Social Power in International Politics. Routledge.

Bandura, A. (1977). Social Learning Theory. Prentice-Hall.

Bar-On, R. (2006). The Bar-On model of emotional-social intelligence (ESI). Psicothema, 18, supl., 13-25.

Bass, B. M. (1990). Bass & Stogdill's Handbook of Leadership: Theory, Research, and Managerial Applications. Free Press.

Bass, B. M., & Bass, R. (2008). The Bass Handbook of Leadership: Theory, Research, and Managerial Applications (4th ed.). Simon & Schuster.

Beattie, W. (1963). A research project in church services to the aging. Review of Religious Research, 4, 104.

Beetham, D. (1991). The Legitimation of Power. Macmillan.

Bergsgard, N. (2018). Power and domination in sport policy and politics - three intertwined levels of exercising power. International Journal of Sport Policy and Politics, 10, 653 - 667.

Blair, C., & Diamond, A. (2007). Biological Systems and the Development of Self-Regulation: Integrating Behavior, Genetics, and Psychophysiology. Journal of Developmental & Behavioral Pediatrics, 28(5), 409-420.

Blanck, P., Hyseni, F., & Wise, F. (2020). Diversity and Inclusion in the American Legal Profession: Workplace Accommodations for Lawyers with Disabilities and Lawyers Who Identify as LGBTQ+. Journal of Occupational Rehabilitation, 30, 537 - 564.

Blass, T. (1981). Obedience to Authority: Current Perspectives on the Milgram Paradigm. Taylor & Francis.

Blau, P. (1964). Exchange and Power in Social Life.

Blau, P. M., & Scott, W. R. (1962). Formal Organizations: A Comparative Approach. Stanford University Press.

Boyer, M. (2004). On the Use of Hierarchies to Complete Contracts When Players Have Limited Abilities.

Brackett, M. A., Rivers, S. E., & Salovey, P. (2011). Emotional intelligence: Implications for personal, social, academic, and workplace success. Social and Personality Psychology Compass, 5(1), 88-103.

Brass, D. J., & Burkhardt, M. (1993). Potential Power and Power Use: An Investigation of Structure and Behavior. Academy of Management Journal, 36(3), 441-470.

Brehm, S. S., & Brehm, J. W. (1981). Psychological Reactance: A Theory of Freedom and Control. Academic Press.

Brophy, J. (2006). History of research on classroom management. In C. M. Evertson & C. S. Weinstein (Eds.), Handbook of classroom management: Research, practice, and contemporary issues (pp. 17-43). Erlbaum.

Brown, M. E., & Mitchell, M. S. (2010). Ethical and unethical leadership: Exploring new avenues for future research. Business Ethics Quarterly, 20(4), 583-616.

Brown, M. E., & Treviño, L. K. (2006). Ethical leadership: A review and future directions. The Leadership Quarterly, 17(6), 595-616.

Bruner, J. S. (1973). The Relevance of Education. Norton.

Burt, R. S. (1992). Structural Holes: The Social Structure of Competition. Harvard University Press.

Canale, M., & Swain, M. (1980). Theoretical bases of communicative approaches to second language teaching and testing. Applied Linguistics, 1(1), 1-47.

Cialdini, R. B. (2007). Influence: The Psychology of Persuasion. Harper Business.

Cornelius-White, J. (2007). Learner-centered teacher-student relationships are effective: A meta-analysis. Review of Educational Research, 77(1), 113-143.

Council of Europe. (2001). Common European Framework of Reference for Languages: Learning, teaching, assessment. Cambridge University Press.

Dahl, R. A. (1961). Who Governs? Democracy and Power in an American City. Yale University Press.

Dearborn, K. (2002). Studies in Emotional Intelligence

Redefine Our Approach to Leadership Development. Public Personnel Management, 31, 523-530.

Decety, J. (2015). The neural pathways, development, and functions of empathy. Current Opinion in Behavioral Sciences, 3, 1-6.

Deutsch, M. (2006). Cooperation and competition. In M. Deutsch, P. T. Coleman, & E. C. Marcus (Eds.), The Handbook of Conflict Resolution: Theory and Practice (pp. 23-42). Jossey-Bass.

Diamond, J. (2016). Power: A User's Guide. Belly Song Press.

Dowding, K. (2006). Three-Dimensional Power: A Discussion of Steven Lukes' Power: A Radical View. Political Studies Review, 4, 136 - 145.

Draganski, B., Gaser, C., Busch, V., Schuierer, G., Bogdahn, U., & May, A. (2004). Neuroplasticity: Changes in grey matter induced by training. Nature, 427(6972), 311-312.

Druskat, V. U., & Wolff, S. B. (2001). Building the emotional intelligence of groups. Harvard Business Review, 79(3), 80-90.

Durlak, J. A., Weissberg, R. P., Dymnicki, A. B., Taylor, R. D., & Schellinger, K. B. (2011). The impact of enhancing students' social and emotional learning: A meta-analysis of school-based universal interventions. Child Development, 82(1), 405-432.

Eagly, A. H., & Carli, L. L. (2007). Through the labyrinth: The truth about how women become leaders. Harvard Business Press.

Elias, M. J., Zins, J. E., Weissberg, R. P., Frey, K. S., Greenberg, M. T., Haynes, N. M., ... & Shriver, T. P. (1997). Promoting social and emotional learning: Guidelines for educators. Association for Supervision and Curriculum Development.

Ely, R. J., Ibarra, H., & Kolb, D. M. (2011). Taking gender into account: Theory and design for women's leadership development programs. Academy of Management Learning & Education, 10(3), 474-493.

Erchul, W., & Raven, B. (1997). Social Power in School Consultation: A Contemporary View of French and Raven's Bases of Power Model. Journal of School Psychology, 35, 137-171

Fast, N. J., Sivanathan, N., Mayer, N. D., & Galinsky, A. D. (2012). Power and overconfident decision-making. Organizational Behavior and Human Decision Processes, 117(2), 249-260.

Fisher, R., Ury, W., & Patton, B. (2011). Getting to Yes: Negotiating Agreement Without Giving In. Penguin Books.

Forrester, J. (1987). Lessons from system dynamics modeling. System Dynamics Review, 3(2), 136-149.

Foucault, M. (1975). Discipline and Punish: The Birth of the Prison. Gallimard.

Foucault, M., Burchell, G., Gordon, C., & Miller, P. (1993). The Foucault effect: studies in governmentality: with two lectures by and an interview with Michel Foucault.

Fox, N. (1998). Foucault, Foucauldians and Sociology. British Journal of Sociology, 49, 415-433.

Freiberg, H. J. (Ed.). (1999). Beyond behaviorism: Changing the classroom management paradigm. Allyn and Bacon.

French, J. R. P., Jr., & Raven, B. (1959). The bases of social power. In D. Cartwright (Ed.), Studies in social power (pp. 150-167). Univer. Michigan.

Frost, D., & Stahelski, A. (1988). The Systematic Measurement of French and Raven's Bases of Social Power in Workgroups.

George, J. (2000). Emotions and Leadership: The Role of Emotional Intelligence. Human Relations, 53(8), 1027-1055.

Gerth, H. H., & Mills, C. W. (Eds.). (1946). From Max Weber: Essays in Sociology. Oxford University Press.

Gillies, R. M. (2003). Structuring cooperative group work in classrooms. International Journal of Educational Research, 39(1-2), 35-49.

Gladwell, M. (2000). The Tipping Point: How Little Things Can Make a Big Difference. Little, Brown and Company.

Goleman, D. (1995). Emotional Intelligence. Bantam Books.

Goleman, D. (1998). What makes a leader? Harvard Business Review, 76(6), 93-102.

Goleman, D. (2006). Social Intelligence: The New Science of Human Relationships. Bantam Books.

Goleman, D., Boyatzis, R., & McKee, A. (2002). Primal Leadership: Learning to Lead with Emotional Intelligence. Harvard Business School Press.

Goussevskaia, O., Kuhn, M., & Wattenhofer, R. (2007). Layers and Hierarchies in Real Virtual Networks.

Grice, H. P. (1975). Logic and conversation. In Syntax and Semantics, 3: Speech Acts (pp. 41-58). Academic Press.

Gross, T. (2023). Development of Theories on Metacognition and Implications on Education. doi: 10.13140/RG.2.2.17395.09769

Gross, T. (2023). Handbook for Higher Education. Vol. 1, Sociodynamics and the Theory of Mind: Scientific Foundations and Principles in Language Proficiency and Communication. Gesis. urn:nbn:de:0168-ssoar-91247-8.

Gross, T. (2023). Handbook for Higher Education. Vol. 2, Linguistic Pragmatics and Contextual Language: Scientific Foundations and Principles in Language Proficiency and Communication. Gesis. urn:nbn:de:0168-ssoar-91014-8.

Haney, C., & Banks, C. (1975). The Stanford Prison Experiment: A Simulation Study of the Psychology of Imprisonment Conducted at Stanford University. Stanford University. Web slide presentation, retrieved from: https://stacks.stanford.edu/file/druid:jj916gd7733/ SC0750s5SPESlide Show Transcript.pdf? download=true

Hartner-Tiefenthaler, M. (2020). Supervisors' power to deal with employees' inner resignation: How perceived power of the organization and the supervisor relate to employees' voluntary and enforced work behavior. European Management Journal, 39, 260-269.

Hattie, J. (2009). Visible Learning: A Synthesis of Over 800 MetaAnalyses Relating to Achievement. Routledge.

Haugaard, M. (2022). Foucault and Power: A Critique and Retheorization. Critical Review, 34, 341 - 371.

Heacox, D. (2002). Differentiating Instruction in the Regular Classroom: How to Reach and Teach All Learners, Grades 3-12. Free Spirit Publishing.

Hoffman, M. L. (2001). Empathy and moral development: Implications for caring and justice. Cambridge University Press.

Hollander, E. P. (1958). Conformity, status, and idiosyncrasy credit. Psychological Review, 65(2), 117-127.

Hollander, J. A., & Einwohner, R. L. (2004). Conceptualizing resistance. Sociological Forum, 19(4), 533-554.

Hur, H. (2020). The role of inclusive work environment practices in promoting LGBT employee job satisfaction and commitment. Public Money & Management, 40, 426 - 436.

Huy, Q. (1999). Emotional Capability, Emotional Intelligence, and Radical Change. Academy of Management Review, 24, 325-345.

Hymes, D. (1972). On communicative competence. In J. B. Pride & J. Holmes (Eds.), Sociolinguistics (pp. 269-293). Penguin Books. Imbusch, P. (2018). Macht - Autorität - Herrschaft. In: Kopp, J., Steinbach, A. (eds) Grundbegriffe der Soziologie. Springer VS, Wiesbaden.

Johnson, D. W., & Johnson, R. T. (1989). Cooperation and competition: Theory and research. Interaction Book Company.

Jordan, P. J., & Troth, A. C. (2004). Managing emotions during team problem solving: Emotional intelligence and conflict resolution. Human Performance, 17(2), 195-218.

Josephs, N., Peng., S., Crawford., F.W. (2022). Communication network dynamics in a large organizational hierarchy. doi: https://doi.org/10.48550/arXiv.2208.01208

Kark, R., & Van Dijk, D. (2007). Motivation to lead, motivation to follow: The role of the self-regulatory focus in leadership processes. Academy of Management Review, 32(2), 500-528.

Kellett, J. B., Humphrey, R. H., & Sleeth, R. G. (2006). Empathy and the emergence of task and relations leaders. Leadership & Organization Development Journal, 27(2), 141-162.

Kelman, H. C. (1958). Compliance, identification, and

internalization: Three processes of attitude change. Journal of Conflict Resolution, 2(1), 51-60.

Keltner, D. (2016). The Power Paradox: How We Gain and Lose Influence. Penguin Books.

Keltner, D., Gruenfeld, D. H., & Anderson, C. (2003). Power, approach, and inhibition. Psychological Review, 110(2), 265-284.

Kern, R. (2000). Literacy and language teaching. Oxford University Press.

Kipnis, D. (1976). The Powerholders. University of Chicago Press.

Knights, D. (2002). Writing Organizational Analysis into Foucault. Organization, 9(4), 575-593.

Knights, D., & Willmott, H. (1989). Power and Subjectivity at Work: From Degradation to Subjugation in Social Relations. Sociology, 23(4), 535-558.

Knudson-Martin, C., Huenergardt, D., Lafontant, K., Bishop, L., Schaepper, J., & Wells, M. A. (2015). Competencies for addressing gender and power in couple therapy: A socioemotional approach. Journal of Marital and Family Therapy, 41(2), 205-220.

Kohn, A. (1992). No contest: The case against competition. Houghton Mifflin.

Kolb, D. M., & Williams, J. (2001). The Shadow Negotiation: How Women Can Master the Hidden Agendas That Determine Bargaining Success. Simon & Schuster.

Laar, C., Meeussen, L., Veldman, J., Grootel, S., Sterk, N., & Jacobs, C. (2019). Coping With Stigma in the Workplace: Understanding the Role of Threat Regulation, Supportive Factors, and Potential Hidden Costs. Frontiers in Psychology, 10.

Lave, J., & Wenger, E. (1991). Situated Learning: Legitimate Peripheral Participation. Cambridge University Press.

Lewicki, R. J., Saunders, D. M., & Barry, B. (1985). Negotiation. McGraw-Hill Education.

Lewin, K., Lippitt, R., & White, R. K. (1939). Patterns of aggressive behavior in experimentally created social climates. Journal of Social Psychology, 10(2), 271-301.

Lindsay, S., Fuentes, K., Ragunathan, S., Lamaj, L., & Dyson, J. (2022). Ableism within health care professions: a systematic review of the experiences and impact of discrimination against health care providers with disabilities.. Disability and rehabilitation, 1-17.

Lopes, P., Salovey, P., Côté, S., & Beers, M. (2005). Emotion regulation abilities and the quality of social interaction. Emotion, 5(1), 113-118.

Loughnan, S., et al. (2013). Revisiting the Stanford prison experiment: Could participant self-selection have led to the cruelty? Personality and Social Psychology Bulletin, 39(6), 791-796.

Lovett, F. (2010). A General Theory of Domination and Justice.

Lukes, S. (1974). Power: A radical view. Macmillan.

Lupton, D. (1995). Perspectives on power, communication, and the medical encounter: Implications for nursing theory and practice. Nursing Inquiry, 2(3), 157-163.

Martin, J. (2016). Emotionally Intelligent Leadership at 30 Rock: What Librarians Can Learn from a Case Study of Comedy Writers. Journal of Library Administration, 56, 345-358.

Martinez-Pons, M. (2000). Emotional Intelligence as a SelfRegulatory Process: A Social Cognitive View. Imagination, Cognition and Personality, 19(4), 331-350.

Martins, M., & Villringer, A. (2018). The human arcuate fasciculus provides specific advantages to process complex sequential stimuli, not hierarchies in general.

Maslach, C. (1996). The Stanford Prison Experiment: Still powerful after all these years. From Kathleen O'Toole. In Stanford University News Service. Retrieved from: https:// news.stanford.edu/pr/97/970108prisonexp.html

Maslow, A. H. (1943). A Theory of Human Motivation. Psychological Review, 50(4), 370-396.

Mayer, J. D., Caruso, D. R., & Salovey, P. (2018). The ability model of emotional intelligence: Principles and updates. Emotion Review, 10(4), 290-300.

Mayer, J. D., Roberts, R. D., & Barsade, S. G. (2008). Human abilities: Emotional intelligence. Annual Review of Psychology, 59, 507-536.

Mayer, J., & Salovey, P. (1993). The Intelligence of Emotional Intelligence. Intelligence, 17, 433-442.

Mehrabian, A. (1972). Nonverbal communication. AldineAtherton.

Men, L. R. (2014). Strategic internal communication: Transformational leadership, communication channels, and employee satisfaction. Management Communication Quarterly, 28(2), 264-284.

Milgram, S. (1963). Behavioral study of obedience. Journal of Abnormal and Social Psychology, 67(4), 371-378.

Milgram, S. (1974). The Perils of Obedience. Harper's Magazine. Retrieved from: https://web.physics.utah.edu/-detar/phys4910/ readings/ethics/PerilsofObedience.html

Mintzberg, H. (1983). Power In and Around Organizations. Prentice-Hall.

Nesler, M., Aguinis, H., Quigley, B., Lee, S., & Tedeschi, J. (1999). The Development and Validation of a Scale Measuring Global Social Power Based on French and Raven's Power Taxonomy. Journal of Applied Social Psychology, 29, 750-769.

Ouchi, W. G. (1979). A conceptual framework for the design of organizational control mechanisms. Management Science, 25(9), 833-848.

Paller, K. A., & Wagner, A. D. (2002). Observing the transformation of experience into memory. Trends in Cognitive Sciences, 6(2), 93-102.

Palmer, B. R., Walls, M., Burgess, Z., & Stough, C. (2001). Emotional intelligence and effective leadership. Leadership & Organization Development Journal, 22, 5-10.

Pekaar, K. A., Bakker, A., van der Linden, D., Born, M. P., & Sirén, H. J. (2018). Managing own and others' emotions: A weekly diary study on the enactment of emotional intelligence. Journal of Vocational Behavior, 2018.

Perales, F., Ablaza, C., Tomaszewski, W., & Emsen-Hough, D. (2021). You, Me, and Them: Understanding Employees' Use of Trans-Affirming Language within the Workplace. Sexuality Research and Social Policy, 19, 760-776.

Piderit, S. K. (2000). Rethinking resistance and recognizing ambivalence: A multidimensional view of attitudes toward an organizational change. Academy of Management Review, 25(4), 783-794.

Pike, K. L. (1982). Linguistic concepts: An introduction to tagmemics. University of Nebraska Press.

Plato. (380 BCE). "The Republic." (B. Jowett, Trans.)

Podsakoff, P., & Schrieshiem, C. (1984). Measurement

and Analytic Shortcomings in Field Studies of French and Raven's Bases of Social Power, 227-231.

Prati, L., Douglas, C., Ferris, G. R., Ammeter, A. P., & Buckley, M. R. (2003). Emotional Intelligence, Leadership Effectiveness and Team Outcomes. International Journal of Organizational Analysis, 11, 21-40.

Rogers, C. R. (1957). The necessary and sufficient conditions of therapeutic personality change. Journal of Consulting Psychology, 21(2), 95-103.

Rogers, C. R., & Freiberg, H. J. (1994). Freedom to learn (3rd ed.). Merrill.

Ryan, R. M., & Deci, E. L. (2000). Intrinsic and extrinsic motivations: Classic definitions and new directions. Contemporary Educational Psychology, 25(1), 54-67.

Salovey, P., & Mayer, J. D. (1990). Emotional intelligence. Imagination, Cognition and Personality, 9(3), 185-211.

Schneider, B., Ehrhart, M. G., & Macey, W. H. (2013). Organizational climate and culture. Annual Review of Psychology, 64, 361-388.

Seligman, M. E. P. (1972). Learned helplessness. Annual Review of Medicine, 23, 407-412.

Sharp, G. (1973). The Politics of Nonviolent Action. Porter Sargent.

Singh, A. P., & Dubey, I. (2015). The Impact of Emotional Intelligence on Team Performance and Learning Organization of Employees. The International Journal of Academic Research in Business and Social Sciences, 7, 304-325.

Slaski, M., & Cartwright, S. (2002). Health performance and emotional intelligence: An exploratory study of retail managers. Stress and Health, 18(1), 63-68.

Slavin, R. E. (1995). Cooperative learning: Theory, research, and practice (2nd ed.). Allyn & Bacon.

Smith, A. (1759). Theory of Moral Sentiments.

Sunindijo, R. Y. (2012). Integrating Emotional Intelligence, Political Skill, and Transformational Leadership in Construction. Clinical and Experimental Dermatology, 14, 182-189.

Swartz, D. (2007). Recasting power in its third dimension. Theory and Society, 36, 103-109.

Sy, T., & Côté, S. (2004). Emotional intelligence: A key ability to succeed in the matrix organization. Journal of Management Development, 23(4), 437-455.

Sy, T., Tram, S., & O'Hara, L. A. (2006). Relation of employee and manager emotional intelligence to job satisfaction and performance. Journal of Vocational Behavior, 68(3), 461-473.

Tåg, J., Åstebro, T., & Thompson, P. (2016). Hierarchies and Entrepreneurship.

Tang, D., Teng, S., Tan, C., Lam, B., & Yuan, C. (2021). Building inclusive workplaces for lesbians and bisexual women in Hong Kong's financial services industry.

Thompson, L. (2009). The Mind and Heart of the Negotiator. Pearson Prentice Hall.

Titchener, E. B. (1909). Lectures on the Experimental Psychology of the Thought-Processes. Macmillan.

Tomlinson, C. A. (2001). How to differentiate instruction in mixed-ability classrooms. Association for Supervision and Curriculum Development.

Tyler, T. R. (2006). Why People Obey the Law. Princeton University Press.

Ury, W., Brett, J., & Goldberg, S. (1988). Getting Disputes Resolved: Designing Systems to Cut the Costs of Conflict. JosseyBass.

Vigoda-Gadot, E., & Meisler, G. (2010). Emotions in Management and the Management of Emotions: The Impact of Emotional Intelligence and Organizational Politics on Public Sector Employees. Public Administration Review, 70, 72-86.

Wartenberg, T. E. (Ed.). (1992). Rethinking Power. State University of New York Press.

Watzlawick, P., Beavin Bavelas, J., & Jackson, D. D. (2011). Pragmatics of Human Communication: A Study of Interactional Patterns, Pathologies and Paradoxes. W. W. Norton & Company. Weber, M. (1922). Economy and Society. University of California Press.

Weber, M. (1947). The Theory of Social and Economic Organization. Free Press.

Wiggins, G., & McTighe, J. (2005). Understanding by Design. ASCD.

Wolff, S. B. (2013). Emotional intelligence and communication in organizations. Journal of Organizational Behavior Management, 33(4), 272-290.

Wong, C., & Law, K. (2002). The Effects of Leader and Follower Emotional Intelligence on Performance and Attitude: An Exploratory Study. Leadership Quarterly, 13, 243-274.

Wrong, D. H. (1995). Power: Its Forms, Bases, and Uses. Transaction Publishers.

Wu, J. (2013). Hierarchy Theory: An Overview.

Xie, L., Chang, C., & Singh, S. (2021). Emotional intelligence, voice and flow: a team-level study of work teams. Team Performance Management: An International Journal.

Zimbardo, P. G. (1973). On the ethics of intervention in human psychological research: With special reference to the Stanford prison experiment. Cognition, 2(2), 243-256.

Zimbardo, P. G. (2007). The Lucifer Effect: Understanding How Good People Turn Evil. Random House.

About the Author

Prof. Dr. Tobey Gross is the head of the International Council of Academics for Progressive Education, which is represented in more than 20 countries on five continents. Based in Germany, he lectures university students in academic research and English language proficiency and cultural sensitivity with an emphasis on communication psychology. While his main research focuses on psycholinguistics and communication, he has also been an international conference speaker on Machine Learning in educational science and is a critical observer of ethics in social media.

www.ingramcontent.com/pod-product-compliance
Lightning Source LLC
Chambersburg PA
CBHW052058270326
41931CB00012B/2800